**New Directions for
Teaching and Learning**

Catherine M. Wehlburg
EDITOR-IN-CHIEF

W9-BHM-702

An Integrative Analysis Approach to Diversity in the College Classroom

Mathew L. Ouellett

EDITOR

Number 125 • Spring 2011
Jossey-Bass
San Francisco

AN INTEGRATIVE ANALYSIS APPROACH TO DIVERSITY IN THE COLLEGE
CLASSROOM
Mathew L. Ouellett (ed.)
New Directions for Teaching and Learning, no. 125
Catherine M. Wehlburg, Editor-in-Chief

Microfilm copies of issues and articles are available in 16mm and 35mm,
as well as microfiche in 105mm, through University Microfilms, Inc.,
300 North Zeeb Road, Ann Arbor, MI 48106-1346.

NEW DIRECTIONS FOR TEACHING AND LEARNING (ISSN 0271-0633, elec-
tronic ISSN 1536-0768) is part of The Jossey-Bass Higher and Adult
Education Series and is published quarterly by Wiley Subscription
Services, Inc., A Wiley Company, at Jossey-Bass, 989 Market Street, San
Francisco, CA 94103-1741. Periodicals postage paid at San Francisco,
CA, and at additional mailing offices. POSTMASTER: Send address
changes to New Directions for Teaching and Learning, Jossey-Bass, 989
Market Street, San Francisco, CA 94103-1741.

New Directions for Teaching and Learning is indexed in CIJE: Current
Index to Journals in Education (ERIC), Contents Pages in Education
(T&F), Current Abstracts (EBSCO), Educational Research Abstracts
Online (T&F), ERIC Database (Education Resources Information
Center), Higher Education Abstracts (Claremont Graduate University),
and SCOPUS (Elsevier).

SUBSCRIPTIONS cost $89 for individuals and $259 for institutions, agencies,
and libraries in the United States. Prices subject to change.

EDITORIAL CORRESPONDENCE should be sent to the editor-in-chief,
Catherine M. Wehlburg, c.wehlburg@tcu.edu.

www.josseybass.com

CONTENTS

SECTION THREE: POINTS OF INTERFACE

SECTION FOUR: INSTITUTIONAL CHANGE

FROM THE SERIES EDITOR

About This Publication

Since 1980, *New Directions for Teaching and Learning (NDTL)* has brought a unique blend of theory, research, and practice to leaders in postsecondary education. *NDTL* sourcebooks strive not only for solid substance, but also for timeliness, compactness, and accessibility.

The series has four goals: to inform readers about current and future directions in teaching and learning in postsecondary education, to illuminate the context that shapes these new directions, to illustrate these new direction through examples from real settings, and to propose ways in which these new directions can be incorporated into still other settings.

This publication reflects the view that teaching deserves respect as a high form of scholarship. We believe that significant scholarship is conducted not only by researchers who report results of empirical investigations, but also by practitioners who share disciplinary reflections about teaching. Contributors to *NDTL* approach questions of teaching and learning as seriously as they approach substantive questions in their own disciplines, and they deal not only with pedagogical issues, but also with the intellectual and social context in which these issues arise. Authors deal on the one hand with theory and research and on the other with practice, and they translate from research and theory to practice and back again.

About This Volume

This volume provides an interdisciplinary forum for educational developers and college and university instructors to describe new frameworks and pedagogical strategies for understanding how a range of aspects of social identity (e.g., race, ethnicity, gender, class, sexual orientation, abilities, religion, etc.) interact in complex and important ways to shape student learning and instructor preparation for creating and sustaining multiculturally inclusive classrooms. Having such an understanding is necessary to transform theoretical understanding and educational practices in today's college and university environments.

Catherine M. Wehlburg
Editor-in-Chief

CATHERINE M. WEHLBURG is the assistant provost for Institutional Effectiveness at Texas Christian University.

EDITOR'S NOTES

Throughout the history of the United States our conceptions of race, gender, and class have morphed alongside changing social and political norms (Omi and Winant, 1994). Education has long been tasked with the challenges of ameliorating social inequities and leveling access to the socioeconomic and political resources of our democratic society (Anderson, 2002; Gordon, 1999; Teddlie and Freeman, 2002). For decades now, higher education institutions have worked consciously to attract a diversity of students and faculty, particularly by gender and race (Association of American Colleges and Universities, 1995).

Related to this end, the research on multicultural education has developed steadily in recent decades. This has been particularly true of resources designed to help instructors in higher education address the social hierarchies and racial contradictions inherent in our society (Adams, Bell, and Griffin, 2007; Morey and Kitano, 1997; Schoem, Frankel, Zúñiga, and Lewis, 1993). Models of stages of identity development (e.g., race, gender, class, sexual orientation, and religion) and social justice (Wijeyesinghe and Jackson, 2001) have been useful in helping to identify, reflect upon, and act to change inequalities in our classrooms and in society (Adams, Bell, and Griffin, 2007; Marchesani and Adams, 1992). In the classroom, they help instructors and students alike to clarify the developmental trajectory of growth in self-knowledge and to see what individuals and groups may, or may not, share in common. Such models also help to juxtapose the individual experience with an illumination of the aggregate experiences of a group and to highlight the systemic nature of hierarchy, group status, and the harm that falls on members of nondominate groups (Adams, Bell, and Griffin, 2007).

The definition of "diversity" has steadily broadened in higher education to include attributes like socioeconomic status and sexual orientation. Although the implications of class status have traditionally been a theme in diversity efforts, Gutmann (2010) in a recent address to university leaders, pointed to wealth, not merit, as the ascendant determinant today of who attends college and where. Campus Pride released the first national report, *2010 State of Higher Education for Lesbian, Gay, Bisexual, and Transgender People*, which surveyed students, faculty, staff, and administrators across the United States about their experiences. The report details significant levels of harassment and discrimination, and makes recommendations for intervention and institutional change (Rankin, Blumenfeld, Weber, and Frazer, 2010).

As we continue to understand such challenges in higher education, an over-focus on single markers of identity formation can inadvertently lead some students to feel that the learning goals and activities at hand are irrelevant or too simplistic to address the questions and concerns important in their lives (e.g., transgender, mixed race, or first-generation immigrant students). Therefore, such approaches to diversity may inadvertently extinguish feelings of inclusion and participation in the learning environment.

What compels us to keep revisiting how to get this right? College and university instructors, even ones who are deeply involved in research, teaching, and service on diversity issues, continue to seek models that help better describe our complex experiences, and enact better strategies for self-reflection, teaching, and learning. Feminist, queer, and ethnic studies scholars continue to put forward compelling arguments for more integrative models of understanding race, class, gender, and sexuality and for centering the experiences of women, people of color, and others traditionally relegated to the margins. Along with the concerns above, we strive to break apart the typically binary constructions of such investigations by including perspectives less often heard.

The genesis for this volume sprang from an academic yearlong faculty and graduate student teaching development effort at the University of Massachusetts Amherst, the Teaching and Learning in the Diverse Classroom Fellows Program (TLDC; Ouellett and Sorcinelli, 1995). The TLDC fellowship offers participants the opportunity to join together in the creative process of fusing the best practices in teaching and learning with an understanding of how to create and sustain classrooms that nurture the success of all students. Initially, the TLDC program brought together an interdisciplinary cohort of faculty and teaching assistant teams to work on individual course design projects.

Over time, I realized that the departmental climate fellows returned to after their TLDC year often stymied their enthusiasm and efforts for innovation. Taking a more systemic approach, I redesigned the TLDC fellowship to be a department-based award. Over the ensuing years, the departments of Journalism, Sport Management, Nutrition, Student Development and Pupil Personnel Services, English, Psychology, Public Health, and Health Studies participated. Among other changes, the new format added support for a department-based diversity project, as well as course innovations.

In 2006–2007, the Women's Studies program (now renamed the Women, Gender, Sexuality Studies program) was chosen for the TLDC program. The faculty and graduate students of the Women's Studies program focused their fellowship year on models of feminist integrative analyses and an exploration of how these models might inform their teaching. Intersectionality marks a movement away from dichotomies to teaching about power and privilege, social justice, and social change from an understanding that race, class, gender, and sexuality are not stand-alone attributes, but

NEW DIRECTIONS FOR TEACHING AND LEARNING • DOI: 10.1002/tl

constellate a complex interwoven dynamic (Weber, 2010). In the last two decades, this model has gained traction well beyond Women's Studies, and applications now extend to disciplines across the humanities, social, and natural sciences (Berger and Guidroz, 2009; Dill and Zambrana, 2009).

Integrative analysis is both a model for understanding the social world and a research method that has grown out of critiques of feminist scholarship and praxis by women of color (Dill and Zambrana, 2009). Rooted in Women's Studies, it is an approach to scholarship, teaching, and activism for social justice. Intersectionality calls for social justice action to combat the economic, social, psychological, and physical violence experienced by those on the margins (Weber, 2010).

Using a collaborative facilitation model, we used seminars to explore a range of integrative feminist models delving into their strengths and challenges for application to teaching, engaged frameworks for multicultural course design, and practiced inclusive pedagogical and classroom management strategies. Based on their interests in applying an integrative analysis about race, class, gender, and sexuality to teaching, research, and community activism, we agreed to blend the seminar with a public lecture series, *Foundations in Feminism*, showcasing feminist research on women of color. The series included both internal and external speakers and topics of domestic violence, reproductive justice, historical accounts of early feminists of color, and progressive feminist perspectives on global economic justice. We also co-funded a speaker on the emergent area of transgender feminism in collaboration with the Stonewall Center, the University of Massachusetts lesbian, gay, bisexual, and transgender organization.

The richness of the year-long TLDC exploration of intersectional analysis galvanized my interest in talking about intersectionality with colleagues from disciplines beyond Women's Studies. In nine chapters, the authors in this volume offer an overview of key tenets of intersectionality and explore applications of this model in faculty and instructional development in higher education. Gathered from across the disciplines, they draw upon a range of approaches to social identity formation, different theoretical models, and a complement of lived experiences. When read together, these chapters offer a systemic approach to change in higher education by addressing innovations at course, department, and institutional levels. Additionally, they offer interdisciplinary program innovations that can support a range of curricular change efforts (i.e., ethnic studies programs, cultural centers, and general education and required college writing courses).

The volume is organized into four sections; nevertheless, all the authors "talk" to each other and central ideas emerge across chapters. Collectively, they make a strong case for the usefulness of intersectionality as an approach to teaching students across the disciplines how to understand, evaluate, and address the complex social issues we face today. Especially important are strategies that engage all of our students on topics that are very often volatile and challenging.

Susan Jones and Charmaine Wijeyesinghe lead Section One of the volume with a historical review of the emergence of intersectional analysis, a highlight of key tenets of the framework, and selected examples of applications in higher education classrooms. Providing further context, C. Shaun Longstreet offers a critique, and an excavation, of the often covert communication and reinforcement of values and behaviors that underlay the formation of a disciplinary identity in Chapter Two.

Examples of course innovation and professional development opportunities that emerge from team teaching are offered in Section Two. Many instructors enter the classroom without the benefit of formal pedagogical training within the discipline, much less a readiness for the challenges of facilitating learning on issues of diversity. In Chapter Three, Jennifer DiGrazia and Elizabeth Stassinos describe what they learned about themselves, their students, and teaching as they reflect on the experience of "practicing publicly" as they used a teaching development grant to renovate their integrated course to incorporate an intersectional approach to diversity. Next, in Chapter Four, Susan M. Pliner, Jonathan Iuzzini, and Cerri A. Banks also examine the positive impact of collaborative teaching teams and the importance of centralized academic administrative support for such innovative endeavors.

Section Three, beginning with Chapter Five by Deborah Carlin, explores the intersectional potential of Queer Theory to guide students' explorations of the intersecting matrices of culture, class, race, ethnicity, nation, and gender in a large lecture setting of a General Education English course. Michel J. Boucher provides a voice for underrepresented and often misunderstood transgender identity issues in Chapter Six. We see how offering students a systems-based and intersectional approach to learning about transgender issues affords an opportunity to unbraid the complexities of gender, sexual orientation, race, and class inequalities from cultural, institutional, and individual perspectives. Educators today are searching for strategies to meet the classroom-based needs of student veterans, refugees, and first-generation immigrants who face issues ranging from marginalization to post-traumatic stress syndrome. In Chapter Seven, Shirley Suet-ling Tang and Peter Nien-chu Kiang describe how pedagogical strategies developed decades ago to meet the needs of Vietnam veterans have evolved into innovative curricular and teaching strategies today. Their chapter offers selected examples of the critical interface refugees and veterans can experience in the classroom for mutual healing and growth. The pedagogical strategies explored in these chapters also offer ideas suitable for interdisciplinary (e.g., General Education and ethnic studies courses) and large lecture settings.

The chapters in Section Four demonstrate how an intersectional approach to faculty and program development can inform institutional change and growth. Faculty learning communities are a well-recognized model useful for providing instructors professional development opportunities. In Chapter Eight, an interdisciplinary cohort of colleagues at Metro State College of Denver (AnnJanette Alejano-Steele, Maurice Hamington, Lunden MacDonald, Mark Potter, Shaun Schafer, Arlene Sgoutas, and Tara Tull) reflects collectively on their experiences in a sustained dialogue using an intersectional approach to understanding diversity. Finally, in Chapter Nine, Cathy Schlund-Vials examines the complexities of teaching about race in a post-racial America and ponders the contributions comparative ethnic studies programs make to institutional change as well individual student learning.

In conclusion, I would be remiss in not acknowledging the limitations of the scope of this volume. Most importantly, it focuses on only one aspect of life in the academy—the teaching and learning environment. For systemic change to become deeply rooted in higher education, all of the executive areas need to be included (Marchesani and Jackson, 2005). Increased institutional support is needed for dialogues across rank, status, and other organizational hierarchies in the academy, even as we seek to deepen and extend interdisciplinarity in academic affairs. Further, we need more opportunities for people of color, women, and lesbian, gay, bisexual and transgender, and other scholars working with intersectionality to gather and talk about their research, teaching, and lived experiences.

Markers of identity are not interchangeable, and a solid foundational knowledge of the historical and cultural factors that have shaped these categories is essential. Advocacy will always have a role in social group relations and education about the discrimination and status differences that continue to inordinately affect women and people of color. Research on sustained democratic outcomes clearly supports a priority on racially diverse learning environments (Gurin, Dey, Hurtado, and Gurin, 2002).

In the end, this volume does not argue for a flattening of differences or for extinguishing research, theory building, and teaching focused on single aspects of social identity. Instead, it argues for another layer of critical analyses that acknowledge the powerful interplay of the many aspects of social identity. Put simply, an over-focus on a single lens of social identity can lead to standoffs rather than sustained dialogues. To rely only on such models will likely not adequately address the rapidly shifting ways in which we talk about and describe identities in society or the complexity of classroom dynamics in the academy today. By illuminating the interconnected nature of systems of oppression, we shine a light on the potential for disrupting the status quo and create stronger alliances for social justice.

Perhaps most importantly, this is not a complete conversation. This collection does not include some important perspectives on higher education campuses today such as the emerging presence of Muslim students, staff, and faculty on campuses or the important pedagogical contributions of community service learning initiatives. Therefore, this volume is an invitation to engage in further collaborative investigation, experimentation, and innovation with an even more diverse constellation of colleagues, students, staff, and community members.

Mathew L. Ouellett
Editor

References

Adams, M., Bell, L. A., and Griffin, P. (eds.). *Teaching for Diversity and Social Justice: A Sourcebook*. 2nd ed. New York: Routledge, 2007.

Anderson, J. D. "Race in American Higher Education: Historical Perspectives on Current Conditions." In W. Smith, P. Altbach, and K. Lomotey (eds.), *The Racial Crisis in American Higher Education*. (rev. ed.) Albany: State University of New York Press, 2002.

Association of American Colleges and Universities. *American Pluralism and the College Curriculum: Higher Education in a Diverse Democracy*. Washington D.C.: Association of American Colleges and Universities, 1995.

Berger, M. T., and Guidroz, K. (eds.). *The Intersectional Approach: Transforming the Academy Through Race, Class, and Gender*. Chapel Hill: The University of North Carolina Press, 2009.

Dill, B. T., and Zambrana, R. E. (eds.). *Emerging Intersections: Race, Class, and Gender in Theory, Policy, and Practice*. New Brunswick, N.J.: Rutgers University Press, 2009.

Gordon, E. W. *Education and Justice: A View from the Back of the Bus*. New York: Teachers College Press, 1999.

Gurin, P., Dey, E. L., Hurtado, S., and Gurin, G. "Diversity and Higher Education: Theory and Impact on Educational Outcomes." *Harvard Educational Review*, 2002, 72(3), 330–367.

Gutman, A. "Leading Universities in the 21st Century: Chances and Challenges." James A. Moffett lecture presented at the Center for Human Values, Princeton University, Princeton, N.J., April 2010. Retrieved August 30, 2010, from http://www.upenn.edu/president/meet-president/moffett-lecture-2010.

Marchesani, L. S., and Adams, M. "Dynamics of Diversity in the Teaching-Learning Process: A Faculty Development Model for Analysis and Action." In L. S. Marchesani and M. Adams (eds.), *Promoting Diversity in the College Classroom: Innovative Responses for the Curriculum, Faculty, and Institutions*. New Directions for Teaching and Learning, no. 52. San Francisco: Jossey-Bass, 1992.

Marchesani, L. S., and Jackson, B. "Transforming Higher Education Institutions Using Multicultural Organizational Development: A Case Study of a Large Northeastern University." In Mathew L. Ouellett (ed.), *Teaching Inclusively: Resources for Course, Department & Institutional Change in Higher Education*. Stillwater, OK: New Forums, 2005.

Morey, A. I., and Kitano, M. K. (eds.). *Multicultural Course Transformation in Higher Education: A Broader Truth*. Boston: Allyn and Bacon, 1997.

Nagda, B. A., Gurin, P., Sorensen, N., and Zúñiga, X. "Evaluating Intergroup Dialogue: Engaging Diversity for Personal and Social Responsibility." *Diversity and Democracy*, 2009, 12(1), 4–6.

Omi, M., and Winant, H. *Racial Formation in the United States: From the 1960s to the 1990s*. (2nd ed.) New York: Routledge, 1994.

Ouellett, M., and Sorcinelli, M. D. "Teaching and Learning in the Diverse Classroom: A Faculty and TA Partnership Program." *To Improve the Academy*, 1995, 14, 205–217.

Rankin, S., Blumenfeld, W. J., Weber, G. N., and Frazer, S. *"Campus Pride's National College Climate Survey: 2010 State of Higher Education for Lesbian, Gay, Bisexual, and Transgender People."* Charlotte, N.C.: Q Research Institute for Higher Education, 2010.

Schoem, D., Frankel, L., Zúñiga, X., and Lewis, E. A. *Multicultural Teaching in the University.* Westport, Conn.: Praeger, 1993.

Teddlie, C., and Freeman, J. A. "Twentieth-Century Desegregation in U.S. Higher Education: A Review of Five Distinct Historical Eras." In W. Smith, P. Altbach, and K. Lomotey (eds.), *The Racial Crisis in American Higher Education.* (rev. ed.) Albany: State University of New York Press, 2002.

Weber, L. *Understanding Race, Class, Gender, and Sexuality.* (2nd ed.) New York: Oxford University Press, 2010.

Wijeyesinghe, C., and Jackson, B. (eds.). *New Perspectives on Racial Identity Development: A Theoretical and Practical Anthology.* New York: New York University Press, 2001.

MATHEW L. OUELLETT *joined the Center for Teaching at the University of Massachusetts Amherst in 1994 and is its director.*

NEW DIRECTIONS FOR TEACHING AND LEARNING • DOI: 10.1002/tl

SECTION ONE

Intersectionality and the Disciplines

1

In this chapter, the authors present key assumptions and tenets of the framework of intersectionality and their relevance and application to college teaching. In addition to discussing several benefits of incorporating intersectionality into teaching, specific strategies for overcoming some of the challenges of teaching from an intersectional perspective are identified. Concrete examples of classroom interventions are given.

The Promises and Challenges of Teaching from an Intersectional Perspective: Core Components and Applied Strategies

Susan R. Jones, Charmaine L. Wijeyesinghe

Introduction

This chapter explores how the framework of intersectionality can be used by faculty in course development and classroom teaching. An overview of intersectionality, highlighting core assumptions and tenets of the framework, is presented first. These assumptions and tenets are then applied to classroom dynamics and the practice of teaching in diverse classrooms. Using scenarios from our own experiences, we then illustrate the promises and challenges of utilizing an intersectional perspective in teaching and advising students. The chapter concludes with thoughts on future directions for the integration of intersectionality into teaching and other areas of faculty work.

Throughout the chapter, we draw on our own experiences of teaching, building theory, and living aspects of intersectionality: specifically, Susan as a faculty member teaching student development theory courses with a long-time research interest in multiple identities, and Charmaine as a consultant in organizational development and social justice who explores the relevance of intersectional theory to racial and multiracial identity models.

New Directions for Teaching and Learning, no. 125, Spring 2011 © Wiley Periodicals, Inc.
Published online in Wiley Online Library (wileyonlinelibrary.com) • DOI: 10.1002/tl.429

Intersectionality: An Overview

Although the term intersectionality is attributed to legal scholar Kimberlé Crenshaw, many intersectional scholars affirm that she gave a name to ideas and practices that had been put in place by scholar-activists long before her publication (Collins, 2009). What Crenshaw argued in her groundbreaking article was that to understand the phenomenon of violence against women of color, the predominating gender-only framework was inadequate. This key premise, that critical social issues cannot be fully understood by focusing on one aspect of identity, or by focusing on multiple identities, held independently while added to each other, is a cornerstone of intersectionality. Early proponents of intersectionality, such as Patricia Hill Collins, pointed out the need to examine the lived experience of marginalized groups, particularly the lives of women of color, through a matrix of domination which necessarily locates individuals within social structures that are interlocking in nature (Collins, 1990). Intersectionality provides educators with an analytic framework for critically evaluating intersecting dimensions such as race, gender, social class, and sexuality in contemporary educational contexts. A core tenet of intersectionality is the connection of these identity dimensions to larger structures of oppression and privilege.

Noting the existence of several definitions of intersectionality, Shields (2008) identified that "a consistent thread across definitions is that social identities which serve as organizing features of social relations, mutually constitute, reinforce, and naturalize one another" (p. 302). Dill and Zambrana (2009) emphasized that intersectionality relates to action, as well as thought, noting that "this work is not seen as emanating solely from a series of linked theoretical propositions, but from an effort to improve society, in part, by understanding and explaining the lives and experiences of marginalized people and by examining the constraints and demands of the many social structures that influence their options and opportunities" (p. 3).

Core Tenets of Intersectionality

Integrating such concepts described above into educational practice is challenging as it may be one thing to understand these ideas in the abstract, and quite another to translate them to a teaching context. This is somewhat ironic, as a central tenet of intersectionality is the insistence on applying theory to practice. However, Dill and Zambrana (2009) describe intersectionality as a framework for integrating analysis, theorizing, advocacy, and pedagogy through their identification of four theoretical interventions. Their use of the term intervention is important and intentional as it conveys the emphasis on action and praxis that underlies intersectionality. These four theoretical interventions not only provide an understanding of the core tenets of intersectionality, but are also transferable to teaching contexts. What follows is a brief overview of each of intersectionality's theoretical interventions. Examples of the applicability of each intervention to a teaching context are given in the next section of the chapter.

Centering the Experiences of People of Color. The experiences of marginalized groups are in the foreground of historical and current intersectional theory and practice, with a specific focus on how race and ethnicity intersect with other categories of identity, such as economic class, gender, and sexual orientation. This centering of the lived experiences of individuals interacting with structures of inequality yields new knowledge that highlights the voices of those individuals and groups previously excluded. An emphasis on counter-narratives illuminates "the relationships of opportunity and constraint created by the dimensions of inequality so that racism, for example, is analyzed not only in terms of the constraints it produces in the lives of people of color, but also in terms of the privileges in creates for Whites" (Dill and Zambrana, 2009, p. 6).

Complicating Identity. An intersectional framework complicates identity by highlighting the complexities of lived experience when a person embodies multiple identities simultaneously that interact and influence each other. These identities are in turn understood in relation to particular and evolving social and political contexts. Further, complicating identity draws attention to the significant diversity within groups and resists essentializing these groups such that this diversity is collapsed into one category. As Dill and Zambrana (2009) point out, "Identity for Latinos, African Americans, Asian, and Native Americans is complicated by differences in national origin or tribal group, citizenship, class (both within the sending and host countries—for recent immigrants), gender as well as race and ethnicity" (p. 7).

Unveiling Power in Interconnected Structures of Inequality. An intersectional framework insists on attention to power and how power operates to shape privilege and oppression. Dill and Zambrana (2009) offer a sophisticated unveiling of power in four interrelated domains: structural (institutions), disciplinary (bureaucratic practices), hegemonic (images, symbols, ideologies that shape social consciousness), and interpersonal (patterns of interaction). Unveiling power highlights the connection between individual identities and larger structures of inequality, as well as the shifting nature of this dynamic given different historical, cultural, and structural contexts (Warner, 2008; Weber, 2010).

Promoting Social Justice and Social Change. An explicit focus and goal of intersectionality is that as the experiences of people of color are foregrounded, identity complicated, and power unveiled, social justice is promoted. As Dill and Zambrana (2009) suggest, "Because intersectional work validates the lives and stories of previously ignored groups of people, it is seen as a tool that can be used to help empower communities and the people in them" (p. 12). They go on to emphasize that this includes not only social action focused on eradicating societal inequalities but also changing the relationship between higher education and society.

The Application of Core Tenets to Teaching and Learning

We now turn to a discussion of the application of the four theoretical interventions of intersectionality to teaching, curriculum development, and classroom dynamics.

Centering the experiences of people of color in intersectional teaching requires a commitment to teach about power and privilege and to use intersectional scholarship and analysis (Dill, 2009). Any academic discipline may be examined through the lens of inequality as could, one might argue, the choice of academic major. For example, analysis of the demographics of those students enrolled in STEM (science, technology, engineering, math) majors is not fully understood by looking at gender alone, but also by race, social class, and high school preparation. Placing students of color at the center of teaching necessitates attention to the content of what is taught as well as adopting different strategies for teaching. Still today, there are examples of well-intentioned faculty who place course material about underrepresented populations in an additive format or as the one week focused on "diversity," instead of integrating the experiences of people of color throughout a semester.

The theoretical intervention concerning the *complicated nature of identity* suggests that those in instructional roles should never presume to know everything about an individual's background or group identity, or if students share a particular group identity that these individuals experience this group identity similarly. For example, a black woman from Uganda will most likely understand herself quite differently (along multiple dimensions of identity) from an African American woman who grew up in the United States, despite the fact that they will both be referred to by others as "black." Teaching and learning strategies such as service learning, problem-based projects, and other innovative methods will help students make connections between theory and practice and think more complexly about the lived experiences of individuals (Dill, 2009).

A commitment to *unveiling power and its relationship to interconnected structures of inequality* in instructional and teaching contexts draws attention to policies, teaching practices, and instructional resources, as well as to the interpersonal practices reflected in how students and faculty treat one another. Dill and Zambrana (2009) provide the example of "everyday racism," situations that are so prevalent that they go unnoticed, such as referring to a white student as a student and an African American student as a black student. At another level, observations about classroom discussions can reveal patterns related to which students speak the most, which ones speak for others, and who remains silent. Power dynamics can also be interrogated through the approach to teaching taken by faculty; for example, whether the faculty member is seen as an expert imparting knowledge to students or whether students and teacher are engaged in a joint process of interrogation and knowledge building.

Faculty are in a unique position to *promote social justice and social change*, the fourth intervention of intersectionality, by intentionally integrating discussions about power and privilege into every course. Some might argue that only certain disciplines lend themselves to intersectional analysis; however, a number of good examples exist highlighting creative approaches, including the use of technology, to engage students in intersectional thinking. Further, faculty can model this approach in the way they conduct their scholarly lives and exhibit their own commitments to social justice.

The Promises and Challenges of Applying Intersectional Interventions in Teaching

This section is organized around four questions that reflect aspects of the interventions discussed earlier. Each question contains both a promise that intersectionality offers teaching and learning, as well as a related challenge. Discussion following each question highlights how intersectionality can be used to realize the promises and overcome the challenges.

Question 1. *If students are viewed as having unique experiences based on their complex and multiple identities, how do faculty acknowledge students' memberships in larger social groups that form the basis of specific forms of oppression and inequality (such as racism, sexism, classism)?*

A core premise of intersectionality is that individuals embody multiple, complex identities that function simultaneously, rather than in isolation of each other (Abes, Jones, and McEwen, 2007; Chen, 2009; Dill, McLaughlin, and Nieves, 2007). However, fundamental to teaching about social identity and social justice is acknowledging that various groups have different experiences in relation to social power and privilege. However, it is our experience that students with limited experience with social justice topics often struggle with core concepts such as power and privilege when discussing identities that traditionally receive social recognition and reward in an unquestioning manner. The tension between an individual orientation toward identity and a group orientation can be seen when a student states that she is just "a person" who happens to be white, heterosexual, able bodied, and Jewish. Often, a student voicing such a perspective would be seen as naive, with little awareness of social oppression, power, and privilege. Although she acknowledges having certain group memberships, such as being white and able bodied, these identities lack meaning and relevance to larger social systems of power and inequality. A different classroom example is when a white, male student discounts the notion that he receives social benefit based on his race because he was raised in a working-class household. Responding to this student only in relation to his experience of his gender or his race discounts the significant ways in which social class interacts with both race and gender.

Compartmentalizing individuals into particular identities (such as race, gender, or sexual orientation) to study one manifestation of oppression (such as racism) runs contrary to attending to the interactive and complicated nature of a person's multiple identities, yet it is very common to do so. Dill, McLaughlin, and Nieves (2007) note that "in the discussion surrounding identity, it is the tension between intersectionality as a tool for illuminating group identities that are not essentialist, and individual identities that are not so fragmentary as to be meaningless, that provides the energy to move the concept forward to the future" (p. 631). This dynamic, evident to different degrees in the student situations described above, presents another challenge of moving students from an individual orientation to identity to a group orientation (which adds the layer of power and privilege).

Attending to multiple, intersecting identities can inhibit students from understanding concepts such as social power and privilege. Luft (2009) indicates that focusing on a single issue, such as race, can be a temporary educational strategy for learners with little previous exposure to anti-racism material. Using intersectionality "strategically and differentially" (Luft, p. 100) and employing single-issue approaches one should consider the needs of learners as well as classroom goals. Fuller use of intersectional concepts can be introduced as the awareness of learners develops, and the class content, structure, and relationships evolve.

Question 2. *How does faculty create space for students to voice their experiences of discrimination and oppression based on identities that have been socially and historically marginalized, while also acknowledging identities where these individuals benefit from and receive social power?*

When students are seen as occupying one social category (such as sexual orientation or economic class) at a time, groups (such as heterosexuals or individuals living in poverty) are often discussed as representing positions of power and privilege or positions of social marginalization and inequality, respectively. This dynamic is particularly evident when specific issues of social justice (e.g., racism, sexism, heterosexism) are taught independently of each other, and can lead to students seeing themselves as only the recipients of power, or the targets of social oppression. Consider this classroom example. During a discussion of an essay by Audre Lorde (1983) in which she notes that there is no hierarchy of oppression, an African American woman with deeply held evangelical Christian beliefs confronts a gay student in the class who tries to draw connections between heterosexism and racism. The African American woman believes that since race is "visible" she cannot help being oppressed, and since sexual orientation is a "choice" to her, she sees no benefit associated with her heterosexual identity.

NEW DIRECTIONS FOR TEACHING AND LEARNING • DOI: 10.1002/tl

A promise of intersectionality is an acknowledgment that each individual inhabits both positions of social privilege and social marginality when all of his or her identities are taken into account. Social power is posited not as something individuals either get or do not get, but as privileges that are both received and denied. Enacting this perspective, faculty can engage the heterosexual, African American student in exploring the prevalence of assumptions related to sexual and gender orientation as a means of developing this student's awareness of the subtle, yet pervasive heterosexual privilege that she receives. Once a foundation for understanding privilege based on heterosexuality is established, this new awareness can be integrated into the student's experience of herself as a black woman. The faculty member teaching the white, male student from the previous question might draw connections between this student's understanding of social marginality based on class background and power and privilege that the student receives due to his race. Once the student grasps the concept of white privilege, the faculty member can use additional material that reflects the voices of people from different oppressed racial groups so that the white student understands racism from a range of perspectives and histories.

Faculty can model personal struggles related to accepting ownership for the concepts of social power and privilege by sharing any self-reflection, reading, and examination concerning identities for which they receive social power and privilege, and those for which they have been targeted. For example, a white, lesbian, Jewish faculty member from a working class background can discuss how her experiences of being marginalized because of sexual orientation, religion, and class influence her identity as a person who receives privilege based on race.

Lastly, Dill (2009) explained, "Inherent in intersectional teaching is a commitment to exploring questions of identity, inequality, and social justice" (p. 245). This commitment requires the ability of faculty to create space for students to share their particular experiences that are based on the confluence of their social identities. Faculty promoting active discussion with their students should develop skills for managing conflict and facilitating difficult dialogues to help students both express diverse opinions, as well as hear experiences that may be vastly different from their own.

Question 3. *How can faculty work collaboratively across disciplines to develop intersectional teaching strategies given the different approaches to identity, teaching methods, and content of various disciplines?*

Developing intersectional teaching strategies and curriculum necessitates the exchange of ideas, teaching practices, and experiences across various disciplines. In addition to developing curriculum that integrates multiple aspects of identity, cooperation across departments such as women's studies, ethnic studies, disability studies, and queer studies yields support networks that are useful in advocating for resources within the larger institution. To be successful in building and sustaining collaborative relationships, faculty from different disciplines can meet regularly to share ways their pedagogy inform the teaching of identity and social justice, as well as methods for teaching any subject to an increasingly diverse student population. The benefits of interdisciplinary scholarship are more widely recognized today and joint appointments more common. Where possible, faculty may consider collaborative research projects, such as faculty from the departments of African American Studies and Queer Studies co-authoring a study of black, gay men.

Question 4. *To what extent, and in what ways does faculty need to demonstrate a personal commitment to enacting social justice to embrace the tenets of intersectionality and integrate this framework into their teaching?*

This question relates to one of the core tenets of intersectionality—the use of the framework to further social justice and social change. Continuous engagement in faculty development opportunities can broaden individual faculty members' awareness of how the dynamics of power and privilege, in the classroom, across the institution, and in the wider society influence the experiences of their students. Institutions can actively support intersectional teaching by offering these types of programs for faculty from all departments. In addition, faculty can seek out other venues, such as informal meetings or lunches with members of other departments, where issues of their own identity as well as strategies for intersectional teaching are explored. The questions posed in this section can be used to begin a conversation concerning integrating intersectionality into teaching.

Future Directions

Intersectionality is gaining currency in a number of educational contexts in part because it makes sense and resonates with the lived experiences of faculty and students alike. This recognition is driving the application of intersectionality to educational practices such as teaching. However, as we look to the future, it is important to acknowledge that we are just beginning to grapple with how such an analytic framework may be applied to day-to-day life in the classroom, and used to dismantle inequality and promote social justice within that classroom, higher education, and larger society.

The framework of intersectionality provides for the analysis of multiple oppression and privileges and recognition that individuals may inhabit both. However, often our gaze is directed toward oppression and oppressed identities. This dynamic is evident in classroom settings, decisions about course content, and scholarship. Intersectional teachers and scholars must be held accountable for exposing structures of both power and privilege, acknowledging the historical roots of intersectionality in the scholarship and lived experiences of women of color, and foregrounding structures of inequality in intersectional analysis.

NEW DIRECTIONS FOR TEACHING AND LEARNING • DOI: 10.1002/tl

Although the constraints of space limited the focus of this chapter to teaching, intersectionality provides renewed support for the practice of grounded, qualitative research, and for research questions that are best served by these methods. Intersectional researchers describe the framework as enabling the interrogation of structures of power and privilege while also illuminating the complexity of the lived experiences of marginalized groups (e.g., Bowleg, 2008; McCall, 2005; Warner, 2008).

The core tenets of intersectionality provide a guiding framework, but not a recipe for application to teaching practice. Adopting an intersectional framework encourages educators to rethink existing practices and ask the question, how might teaching look different if an intersectional approach is taken? Or how might existing theories or models for understanding students or classroom environments be different if intersectionality were taken into account? We hope this chapter provides the guidance needed to begin to engage with such questions and examine their teaching practice through the tenets of centering the experiences of people of color, complicating identity, unveiling power, and promoting social change. As the identification of promises and challenges illustrates, this is not easy work, but it is essential work for those who are committed to promoting equity and inclusion through teaching and learning.

References

Abes, E. S., Jones, S. R., and McEwen, M. K. "Reconceptualizing the Model of Multiple Dimensions of Identity: The Role of Meaning-Making Capacity in the Construction of Multiple Identities." *Journal of College Student Development*, 2007, 48, 1–22.

Bowleg, L. "When Black + Lesbian + Woman ≠ Black Lesbian Woman: The Methodological Challenges of Qualitative and Quantitative Intersectionality Research." *Sex Roles*, 2008, 59, 312–325.

Chen, G. A. "Managing Multiple Social Identities." In N. Tewari and A. N. Alvarez (eds.), *Asian American Psychology: Current Perspectives*. New York: Psychology Press, 2009.

Collins, P. H. *Black Feminist Thought: Knowledge, Consciousness, and the Politics of Empowerment*. Boston: Unwin Hyman, 1990.

Collins, P. H. "Foreword: Emerging Intersections—Building Knowledge and Transforming Institutions." In B. T. Dill and R. E. Zambrana (eds.), *Emerging Intersections: Race, Class, and Gender in Theory, Policy, and Practice*. New Brunswick, N.J.: Rutgers University Press, 2009.

Dill, B. T. "Intersections, Identities, and Inequalities in Higher Education." In B. T. Dill and R. E. Zambrana (eds.), *Emerging Intersections: Race, Class, and Gender in Theory, Policy, and Practice*. New Brunswick, N.J.: Rutgers University Press, 2009.

Dill, B. T., McLaughlin, A. E., and Nieves, A. D. "Future Directions of Feminist Research: Intersectionality." In N. Hesse-Biber (ed.), *Handbook of Feminist Research*. Thousand Oaks, Calif.: Sage, 2007.

Dill, B. T., and Zambrana, R. E. "Critical Thinking About Inequality: An Emerging Lens." In B. T. Dill and R. E. Zambrana (eds.), *Emerging Intersections: Race, Class, and Gender in Theory, Policy, and Practice*. New Brunswick, N.J.: Rutgers University Press, 2009.

Lorde, A. *There Is No Hierarchy of Oppressions*. New York: Council on Interracial Books for Children, 1983.

Luft, R. E. "Intersectionality and the Risk of Flattening Difference: Gender and Race Logics, and the Strategic Use of Antiracist Singularity." In M. T. Berger and K. Guidroz (eds.), *The Intersectional Approach: Transforming the Academy through Race, Class, & Gender.* Chapel Hill, N.C.: The University of North Carolina Press, 2009.

McCall, L. "The Complexity of Intersectionality." *Signs: Journal of Women in Culture and Society,* 2005, *30*, 1771–1800.

Shields, S. "Gender: An Intersectionality Perspective." *Sex Roles,* 2008, *59*, 301–311.

Warner, L. R. "A Best Practices Guide to Intersectional Approaches in Psychological Research." *Sex Roles,* 2008, *59*, 454–463.

Weber, L. *Understanding Race, Class, Gender, and Sexuality: A Conceptual Framework.* (2nd ed.) New York: Oxford University Press, 2010.

SUSAN R. JONES, is an associate professor in the higher education and student affairs program at The Ohio State University.

CHARMAINE L. WIJEYESINGHE is a consultant in organizational development, social justice, and multiracial identity development residing in Delmar, New York.

2

The author advocates for greater attention to the unspoken, and potentially repressive, dynamics that faculty may rely upon to cultivate a disciplinary identity in the classroom. Being transparent and critically reflective about the language, ideas, and practices employed in class will empower students and augment their cognitive abilities in new ways.

The Trouble with Disciplining Disciplines

C. Shaun Longstreet

In this chapter, I focus on intersectionality as a heuristic means toward an open and affirming classroom and as a model grounded in a larger history of calls for anti-oppressive pedagogy. In the wake of the Second World War, there was a groundswell of intellectual change globally: post-colonial thought, liberation theology, and the larger post-modern movement raised critical awareness about structures of socio-economic power and the cultural institutions that supported them. Many philosophers and activists associated with post-war social and political movements have framed education as a means to combat poverty and empower the working class. Education, as an institution and a practice, became a pillar of human rights and a path towards greater agency no longer reserved for elites.

Three critical pivots set the background to this piece. The first is Paolo Freire, who clearly connected social justice with pedagogy and contended that teaching itself is a political act. In his work, he encouraged students and teachers to develop a critical consciousness that raised awareness of the cultural narratives propagating structures of privilege and suppression (Freire, 1970). Although some cultural critics noted how education could create agency, others pointed to ways in which education could be a tool for oppression, and this marks the second pivot for this chapter. For example, Henry Giroux censured what he saw as the positivist culture within education. He tasked a pedagogical culture wherein socio-political elites promoted particular narratives of knowledge as concrete truths to preserve a repressive status quo (Giroux, 1981). The call for being responsive to underrepresented students and valuing diverse experiences as a means for more equitable and inclusive campuses forms the third pivot here. As the

NEW DIRECTIONS FOR TEACHING AND LEARNING, no. 125, Spring 2011 © Wiley Periodicals, Inc.
Published online in Wiley Online Library (wileyonlinelibrary.com) • DOI: 10.1002/tl.430

civil rights movement led to more accessibility, post-secondary institutions saw the rise of more diverse student populations. Subsequently, faculty and administrators have increasingly recognized the benefits of, and challenges to, adjusting higher education to meet the needs of the varied populations coming to campuses (Ouellett, 2010).

As diverse voices continued, and continue, to struggle for social justice, they have further refined the recognition of how personal experience and social location are factors in pedagogy. Feminists, race theorists, and queer theorists have long contended that if education is to serve social justice fully, then all aspects of systemic domination need to be considered (hooks, 1994; Kumashiro, 2002). They consistently highlight how particular aspects of social identity (for example, race, sexuality, gender, ability, socio-economic status) serve as an ever-present means to organize interpersonal relationships and access to power. An intersectional analysis suggests that these aspects are neither static, nor exclusive from one another; rather they are interdependent and mutually inform a greater whole (Collins, 2000; Knudsen, 2006). Recognizing the dynamic relationships between various components of social identity as they affect one's social location and access to socio-economic power has come to be known as *intersectionality*.

In addition to highlighting the interdependence of social categories such as race, gender, and sexuality, intersectionality emphasizes that social identity is performative; people actively claim aspects of identity for themselves and project expectations of identity onto others (Collins, 2000; McCall, 2003; Shields, 2008). Moreover, intersectionality theorists, in step with other post-modern culture critics, highlight the pervasiveness of identity politics in knowledge production. Because the academy has traditionally been the domain of abled, white, heterosexual, male privilege, it has tended to reflect the values and interests of that demographic, often to the detriment of other social groups (Knudsen, 2006).

In this chapter, I draw from intersectionality to investigate identity development in the classroom. I explore the ramifications of how instructors encourage students to "perform" a constructed pattern of thoughts, actions, and values in the classroom, a pattern we can call a disciplinary or professional identity. Although the work here calls attention to the potential problems that can arise from unreflective identity formation in any classroom, it specifically explores how the application of intersectionality played out in a religious studies curriculum that actively promoted a more socially just campus. My own practice in the classroom centers on teaching religious studies courses in post-secondary education, primarily comparative religion and biblical studies. My work at Texas A&M University (TAMU; College Station, Texas) from 2004–07, where I received an internal faculty development grant to "queer the religious studies curriculum," will serve as part of my case for drawing upon intersectionality for an open and affirming classroom.

Disciplining Disciplines

Scholars in any specific field compartmentalize their work vis-à-vis other scholars and they advocate particular lines of thought and methodologies. They carve spaces for themselves within a broader spectrum of the sciences, humanities, and social sciences by producing knowledge along historically conditioned modes of thought and practice. For example, a sociologist is distinct from an anthropologist in the types of knowledge each will develop over their academic careers. Likewise, a physical anthropologist who studies hominid evolution is distinct from a cultural anthropologist who studies linguistic patterns in Appalachia. It is more than a difference in data sets, however. Disciplinary communities have particular histories, values, practices, and institutions that distinguish them from one another, and these differences are communicated to students in the classroom. One's professional or disciplinary identity hangs upon subscribed patterns of thoughts, actions, and values shared with similar academics who circulate in particular institutions attending to similar types of data.

When faculty members teach, they propagate a professional identity in their classrooms built upon, and designed to advance, their particular academic discipline. Subsequently, from the beginning of a course through to the last class, an instructor teaches students to follow in her or his academic footsteps. Through practice and recitation, students internalize the rhetoric of their faculty's discipline, learning to conform to a professional or disciplinary identity. Faculty cultivates a professional identity partially by explicitly communicating some of their discipline's rhetoric explicitly with certain stated benchmarks. At the same time, many other discipline markers are only implicitly communicated in terms of faculty response to students in the classroom and to their submitted work. In either case, faculty establishes a frame of beliefs, narratives, practices, and institutions within which it is expected that students will participate. The stated or implied goal of this expectation is the successful completion of the course and/or further participation in that academic discipline. For example, a historian models a set of approaches to written records and the ways in which one can interpret them; students then research primary and secondary sources attempting to apply their newly learned skills as budding historians. That this practice has pedagogical value is not a point of contention. Promoting a skill set within a limited arrangement of disciplinary parameters is a typical method for constructivist approaches to education (for example, Middendorf and Pace, 2004).

Conforming to a disciplinary identity often involves significant unspoken processes, and it occurs without much effort because faculty and students both are already well suited to giving and receiving social cues that express "belonging." Having acted upon common expressions of social identity long before coming into a course, it is reasonable to expect that both instructor and students in a teaching and learning environment exercise these patterns without much thought to communicate a sense of belonging. Neither the students nor the faculty come to the classroom as blank slates; as intersectional theory indicates, they are already conversant with expressions of personal identity in terms of categories such as race, class, gender expression, ability, and sexuality (Abes and Jones, 2004; Shields, 2008). Problems can arise, though, when patterns of social privilege or marginalization are grafted upon a disciplinary identity, either as a means for classroom management or unreflective assumptions about the discipline itself. If instructors want to avoid creating a disciplinary identity developed from implicit patterns of social normativity, they must actively seek to root out institutionalized racist, homophobic, sexist, ableist, and classist pressures within their pedagogy (Acker, 2005). Assumptions brought upon an uncritically developed disciplinary identity can blur identity politics with the actual skills required to perform a particular line of research. Such occurrences will stunt the potential of all students at best, but at worst it will reinforce the exclusion and oppression of under-represented and traditionally silenced students.

By definition, reductionist approaches to one's discipline model exclusivist patterns of thought and behavior. If an instructor relies too heavily on a reductionist stance as part of cultivating or policing a disciplinary identity, she or he does not promote much learning beyond rote habit. Practices and narratives about the discipline become internalized as "common sense," requiring participation by all without question because of an implied nature of truth about them. This promotes a regime of normativity that encourages a silent socialization wherein course activities take on an unquestioned legitimacy and instructors police the classroom with the presentation that what is done there is a matter of assumed truth (Acker, 2005; Shields, 2008).

Aside from reducing authentic engagement, the creation of normativity in a course is further problematized when sexuality, race, class, and gender already condition the norms of a discipline. Historically, academic disciplines already reflect the interests of those who are socially privileged. Unreflective approaches to the formation of a disciplinary identity in the classroom can pick up harmful patterns of identity expression and the accompanying patterns of marginalization. As knowledge production has primarily been in the hands of white elite men, the parameters of research and disciplinary identities have presumed a normative posture from those perspectives (Zambrana and Dill, 2009). When a student joins a class, the group dynamic posed by the faculty and other students will project an expectation to take on a disciplinary identity. Consequently, those bodies that more quickly reflect the historical values and interests of the discipline are likelier to succeed and feel a sense of inclusion. Those bodies that do not will retain a sense of continued marginalization; their interests will neither be reflected nor valued, and they are less likely to succeed (Gurin, Dey, Hurtado, and Gurin, 2002).

NEW DIRECTIONS FOR TEACHING AND LEARNING • DOI: 10.1002/tl

Intersectionality Applied to Religious Studies

Having explored how intersectionality can highlight potential problems of uncritical curriculum development, let us turn to how these theories can help faculty and administrators create a more socially just space in higher education. As mentioned above, I will use my experience at TAMU as a case in point. This is not to set my experience as a model for success; rather it is to provide an example of the application of some of the concepts discussed and reveal more of my own positionality as I wrote this chapter.

Intersectionality, as an approach to identity, calls attention to the multiplicity within personal identity, but it also calls practitioners to act. There are many components of one's sense of self—often tied to social power and to categories of thinking. My position in the course as a white, English-speaking, able-bodied, male instructor was visible to the class when I walked in. Because of my role in the classroom, I also made visible my identification as a gay, Canadian, first-generation college student with a doctorate in theology from a Catholic university. At the same time, I explicitly did not reveal my personal religious affiliation. I self-identified as gay to highlight that there was a diversity in the classroom that some might not have expected for someone teaching biblical studies or comparative religions, thereby blurring or even negating the equation of a disciplinary identity with any particular type of body, class, or sexuality. I explained to the students that I did not reveal my personal faith perspective because I was modeling a parameter of behavior for the classroom—that in a historical–critical religious studies approach to religion, we would frame our discussions about religious beliefs from a third-person perspective. The point of doing this was twofold. First, it created a space for greater neutrality whereby the pressure to "witness" one's personal faith in the classroom was no longer appropriate. Second, it raised a student's consciousness about a different way to approach religion and forced her or him to reflect on what it might feel like to have other people talk about her or his personal faith. This allowed us to talk more critically about Christianity, and class discussions about other religious traditions had far less supersessionist or orientalist tones.

The university enrollment at TAMU's main campus is predominantly white, traditional college aged, middle class, and has a reputation for being politically conservative with a large evangelical Protestant population. The great majority of students who came into the religious studies classroom shared similar outlooks regarding their assumptions of religion as something that was very public, highly performative, and almost radically normative. This posed problems for developing buy-in from the majority students and for creating a space where non-majority students could feel more comfortable to engage with their points of view. Because people tend to base new knowledge on what is already known, developing a disciplinary identity for students had to occur with attention given to avoiding importing social patterns that serve to maintain privilege for some and replicate marginal stations for others. When considering the variety of backgrounds and experiences held by students in my classroom, it was fruitful to think about destabilizing the normativity of a disciplinary identity because it could disrupt preconceptions about academic approaches to religion that many students had upon entering the classroom.

Intersectionality points to the varietal and performative condition of identity, and queer theory further deconstructs assumptions about the components of identity (Kumashiro, 2002; Shields, 2008). Drawing upon queer notions of identity, the students and I in each course that I taught would identify a spectrum of what our professional identity could consist, in how we could set ourselves apart from academics in other fields who studied religious phenomena. Finally, we began to define the terms and data sets that could inform our professional identity. We drew the horizon, or spectrum, of religious studies, identifying one pole of the spectrum as insider/theological and the other pole as outsider/phenomenological. Because students participated in creating the context and conditions of our work, they were more prepared to critically approach texts and ideas that required high levels of critical engagement. At the same time, neither extremity of the spectrum was framed as right or wrong, but rather as more or less appropriate for a given context. This allowed students to recognize their personal position along the spectrum, while being able to accept the range of approaches we would use within the context of the course. Explicit identity development where self is negotiated then created increased opportunities for complex meaning-making (Abes and Jones, 2004; Epstein, O'Flynn, and Telford, 2003).

During the course of a semester, we worked to avoid invoking social patterns frequently used to suppress difference or dissent (cf. Acker, 2005). One step towards creating a professional identity that is less biased towards one particular race, class, and gender was to be cognizant of the examples used during the course of instruction. Implicit use of one particular category as an "inclusive universal" implies the assumption of its normativity. For example, gender neutrality points towards the male, and the raceless race is white. Otherwise, when gender is made explicit, it is to stress the female, just as other categorical facets of identity are invoked to register something other than abled, white, heterosexual, and middle-class (Knudsen, 2006). Another way of avoiding implying normativity for specific social groups within one's professional identity was in thinking about the activities that students are asked to perform. For example, assigning time-intensive group work that ignores familial or financial obligations outside of the classroom contributes to a professional identity that normalizes the middle class, the abled, and men since they most often have the opportunity and flexibility to succeed under such requirements. Instead, students were required to read texts on their own and class time was used for interactive learning.

Applying the modes of thinking that intersectionality raises to a disciplinary identity can help faculty make clear what might have gone unstated about the creation of what makes someone a professional in a particular field. In being more deliberate in naming the processes, the lines of thinking, and the institutions of their disciplines, instructors can develop a sharper vision of their work for students. Explicitly identifying the approach one takes to participate in the constructed identity of "religious studies scholar" allowed students to approach the discipline without a rigid, reductionist identity. Instead of creating a binary choice of religious studies scholar/non-religious studies scholar, it was important for me to communicate a professional character that is constructed around specific, relevant skills that resemble the work patterns of other religious studies scholars. This created more opportunities to root out historically informed, but irrelevant biases in defining that disciplinary identity.

Stressing the constructed nature of disciplinary thought and practice created space for greater participation for the students because they observed how they were constructing knowledge. When an instructor indicates how the discipline consists of particular practices, theories, and institutions that play upon each other, students could see a larger context for themselves within that discipline. Likewise, it is important to be aware that these practices, theories, and institutions are shifting over time; that they are not static truths, but are continually informed and reformed by new information. Making students aware of the multiple factors that go into creating a disciplinary identity invites them to take a more active role in participating in the creation and further refinement of that identity. By complicating the professional identities being cultivated in a classroom, faculty can be more effective in developing students' cognitive abilities. When faced with alterity, students are more likely to foster increased cognitive complexity (Gurin, Dey, Hurtado, and Gurin, 2002). In the religious studies courses, we spent a significant amount of time over the course of the semester evaluating and re-evaluating what someone might consider a religious phenomenon. This continually refocused students' attention on how a line of disciplinary practices, thoughts, and institutions depend on framing, thereby prompting them to make critical choices and reflect on their own intellectual development.

Instructors can cultivate a professional identity in the classroom that is neither specious nor lax. Having a non-normative professional identity does not mean a free-for-all in a course or that classrooms should lack standards or assessment. Students in TAMU comparative religions courses were held to high expectations, and a consistent point of course evaluation feedback was the course workload. If instructors think about patterns of interaction in the classroom, they should be explicit in expressing a range of appropriate behaviors. They must be clear, to themselves and to their students, as to why they expect some behaviors and not others. Faculty can cultivate a particular set of skills that, for convenience or context, provide a disciplinary label. Giving a reasoned and purposeful explanation to the approaches to one's work is quite different from outlining sanctions for actions outside of a normative approach to a set discipline. Having a clear sense of approach and thought will allow instructors to better hone in on the necessary skills for the completion of course goals.

Conclusion

In this chapter, I challenge faculty and administrators to be more aware of the processes that are involved with creating a disciplinary identity in the classroom. Unexamined inferences about race, socio-economic status, sexuality, and gender identity in the formation of a disciplinary identity can replicate patterns of marginalization found outside the classroom. Intersectionality has introduced a critical space that fosters an environment that avoids replicating pressures of alienation that many non-majority students already face. By highlighting disruptions in theory and practice, instructors can destabilize recurring patterns of social normativity and create space for the non-normative in our classrooms. By thinking about a professional identity that is both conditional and historically conditioned, instructors and students can better limit socialized patterns of privilege and marginalization, establish a more inclusive environment, and inhabit a more effective space for critical thinking.

References

Abes, E. S., and Jones, S. R. "Meaning-Making Capacity and the Dynamics of Lesbian College Students' Multiple Dimensions of Identity." *Journal of College Student Development*, 2004, *45*(6), 612–632.

Acker, J. "Inequality Regimes: Gender, Class, and Race in Organizations." *Gender & Society*, 2005, *20*(4), 441–464.

Collins, P. H. *Black Feminist Thought: Knowledge, Consciousness, and the Politics of Empowerment*. New York: Routledge, 2000.

Epstein, D., O'Flynn, S., and Telford, D. *Silenced Sexualities in Schools and Universities*. London: Trentham Books, 2003.

Freire, P. *Pedagogy of the Oppressed*. New York: Herder and Herder, 1970.

Giroux, H. *Ideology, Culture and the Process of Schooling*. Philadelphia: Temple University Press, 1981.

Gurin, P., Dey, E., Hurtado, S., and Gurin, G. "Diversity and Higher Education: Theory and Impact on Educational Outcomes." *Harvard Educational Review*, 2002, *72*(3), 330–366.

hooks, b. *Teaching to Transgress*. London: Routledge, 1994.

Knudsen, S. "Intersectionality—A Theoretical Inspiration in the Analysis of Minority Cultures and Identities in Textbooks." In É. Bruillard, B. Aamotsbakken, S.V. Knudsen, and M. Horsley (eds.), *Caught in the Web or Lost in the Textbook? STEF, IARTEM IUFM de Basse-Normandie*. Paris: Jouve, 2006.

Kumashiro, K. *Troubling Education: Queer Activism and Antioppressive Pedagogy*. New York: Routledge Falmer, 2002.

McCall, L. "The Complexity of Intersectionality." *Signs: Journal of Women in Culture and Society*, 2003, *30*(3), 1771–1800.

Middendorf, J., and Pace, D. "Decoding the Disciplines: A Model for Helping Students Learn Disciplinary Ways of Thinking." *New Directions for Teaching and Learning*, 2004, *98*, 1–12.

Ouellett, M. L. "Overview of Diversity Issues Relating to Faculty Development." In K. H. Gillespie and D. Reimondo (eds.), *A Guide to Faculty Development.* (2nd ed.) San Francisco: Jossey-Bass, 2010.

Shields, S. A. "Gender: An Intersectionality Perspective." *Sex Roles*, 2008, *59*, 301–311.

Zambrana, R. E., and Dill, B. T. "Conclusion: Future Directions in Knowledge Building and Sustaining Institutional Change." In B. T. Dill and R. E. Zambrana (eds.), *Emerging Intersections; Race, Class, and Gender in Theory, Policy and Practice.* New Brunswick, N.J.: Rutgers University Press, 2009.

C. SHAUN LONGSTREET is coordinator of educational enhancement at the University of Texas at Dallas.

SECTION TWO

Collaborative Teaching

Two instructors, one from the English department and one from the Criminal Justice department, describe how, using intersectional analysis as a model, they moved from a "linked" to an "integrated" design for a co-taught Criminal Justice course for first-year students. They describe the evolution of the struggle with and strategies for addressing issues of culture, power, and identity within the courses.

The Writers and the Detectives: Cultural Difference, Identity, and Pedagogical Disciplines in an Integrated Classroom

Jennifer DiGrazia, Elizabeth Stassinos

Student resistance to critical thinking emblematic of a liberal arts curriculum is often painfully obvious in freshman writing classes that impose a process-based approach to writing and thinking. Despite enrollment in a small northeastern rural and residential state liberal arts college (recently, university), our students tend to be first-generation, local, and regional high school graduates and non-traditional students who are returning to school. Except for the relatively small percentage of liberal arts students who are looking for value for the dollar, most of our students resist what Philip Eubanks and John D. Schaeffer (2008) refer to as "academic bullshit" in their article, "A Kind Word for Bullshit: The Problem of Academic Writing." Criminal justice students, like their peers in other majors with strong vocational orientations, often resist taking any more than the required liberal arts courses. In fact, they tend, by interest and vocation, to gravitate toward Criminal Justice (CJ) electives to meet our college's core and disciplinary requirements.

The Institutional and Disciplinary Contexts

In many key courses, CJ majors get little exposure to writing and revision as forms of critical thinking and as part of their assessment—an issue in

NEW DIRECTIONS FOR TEACHING AND LEARNING, no. 125, Spring 2011 © Wiley Periodicals, Inc.
Published online in Wiley Online Library (wileyonlinelibrary.com) • DOI: 10.1002/tl.431

many Criminal Justice departments, not one only specific to ours. Professors who want to teach criminology as a "science" often rely heavily on statistics, which are emphasized in state and federal grants and police work. Writing as praxis is an exception. Statistics in criminology is a way to bolster the reputation of a field that wants very badly to be viewed as a science and as separate from the subjectivity and researcher's bias that many believe characterize the liberal arts. Thus, CJ professors often opt for multiple choice exams as a way to test their version of statistical "truths" (which are hard to know, when likely half of all crimes are not reported, the often hetero-normative and murky unknowns of "motive" and "facts."

At our institution, CJ students take classes in their major in a building that is about a mile from the main campus, isolated against a beautiful park. Although the view is pastoral, the students are further isolated by the fact that the gender ratio in classes are 60:40 male to female and further divided by the sometimes dueling ethos of the two disciplines. Many students come to the CJ major with crime scene investigation job hopes even though (1) forensics is not likely to employ our students without many years more of lab science training; and (2) local, state, and federal law enforcement job recruiters want good writers and students with bilingual/cultural expertise and computer skills. In addition, they will be disappointed almost immediately in their job hunt because, as has been the case for many years, the job market has dropped out of the bottom of many policing departments in the Northeast due to a glut of students and programs and the recession–economy, as well as the state and local hiring freezes of 2009–10.

Disciplines and Identities

Although most composition scholars resist the tendency of some in other disciplines who believe that composition courses are meant to serve other disciplines (often so that those teaching in other disciplines do not have to do the work of writing instruction), it is fair to say that one purpose introductory composition courses serve is to be "gateway" courses, places where students are initiated into the norms, language, and ways of thinking associated with academic writing. Since its inception in the 1970s, Writing Across the Curriculum (WAC) scholarship has been linked to studies in composition and rhetoric, and because most composition programs are housed in English departments, composition continues to work to establish itself as a field of inquiry and scholarship in its own right. In addition to building consensus about the role that writing and writing instruction should play in the academy, WAC scholarship often examines the tension between writing that is discipline-specific and writing for other more general and public audiences. As Anne Herrington and Marcia Curtis note in *Persons in Process: Four Stories of Writing and Personal Development in College* (2000), in the process of their case study research, they "were struck by the contrasting and sometimes conflicting demands that these first-year students were called upon to negotiate (and by the truly slippery nature of "academic" writing, if it is to be defined by what is actually written in today's academy). As Herrington and Curtis suggest, the idea of academic writing and academic norms is contentious and variable across disciplines and sometimes between instructors within disciplines. So, of course, such a purpose immediately raises the question of which norms, which disciplines, and which language?

In fact, our colleagues in many disciplines, not just CJ, are opposed to what they see as the time-consuming grading of students' writing. They see this as "the English department's job." With few exceptions, writing is too often not considered as one tool among many for assessment in CJ. This is true even as most professors acknowledge the importance of observation analysis, the "literacy" necessary for good investigative detective work, much less legal protocols. Although most CJ professors respect the future power that 22-year-old students will have as officers with guns, whose interpretations and police discretion will often be their only rationale for action in their work with the public, they may not connect writing and the critical thinking that drives and results from revision to the creation of those same students' development of interpretation, analysis, or keen legal judgment.

Jen, as a compositionist visiting the discipline of Criminal Justice, revised her expectations about authority, fostering classroom community and structuring writing assignments in ways that more clearly helped students and her to grapple with issues of power and authority (her own and each student as a writer and as a civil servant) as well as the ways the interactions between Elizabeth and herself were influenced by shared authority, gender norms, assumptions, and heteronormativity (the belief system that sustains the power associated with heterosexual privilege and that excludes people and communities that do not subscribe to white, heterosexual privilege). Elizabeth contends essay and daily writing explorations have completely changed her teaching pedagogy as an anthropologist teaching criminology.

As a way to approach this subject matter, Elizabeth had struggled with the heteronormative "Just the facts ma'am" approach of the discipline of Criminal Justice research against her own training in the politics and the "discretionary" and interpretive practices of student learners.

Beyond texts, she suggests that CJ faculty may be hesitant to raise questions about power and authority generally. Like other professional programs, they may feel the need to prove their academic standing—that way what they do is "real" and central to the university mission. In fact, when she first started working in the Criminal Justice department she was told that the department "kept the lights on" in the college because the major was so big. Add to this the issue of "insider status" in the Criminal Justice field. Perceived legitimacy is often based on one's field experiences, professional affiliations, or ties to federal, state, and regional justice agencies. Add to this the gender issues within the Criminal Justice department.

Colleagues and students can engage Elizabeth's critique of the narrow sociologically defined and heteronormative norms of the department, and perhaps the discipline, because of the complex intersections of her identity. She is one of only a few women in the Criminal Justice department, serves as an affiliate faculty member in Ethnic and Gender Studies, and is one of only a dozen or so "out" faculty members on campus. As a person who volunteered in prison writing rehabilitation programs and whose father was a celebrated FBI agent (whose cases are documented in two books, *Nightmover: How Aldrich Ames Sold the CIA to the KGB for $4.6 million* (Wise, 1995) and *Spy: The Inside Story of How the FBI's Robert Hanssen Betrayed America* (Wise, 2003), Elizabeth could "belong" to the CJ department as a "real" and a legitimate authority for students in a way that Jennifer, from English Composition, could not.

Being a queer faculty member with affiliate status in the proposed Ethnic and Gender Studies department might also have also influenced her to conform more to what she saw as CJ disciplinary practices. We think this is a common problem when the faculty is trying to integrate themselves and gain respect for their teaching and service work.

Unlike other composition classes Jen had taught, this one was comprised almost entirely of white, working- and middle-class men who had a fascination with guns and authority. One example illustrates the divide and the differences in the disciplinary conventions. On the first day the class met, we began the CJ section with a brief overview of the theories that would inform the course and the literature we would read. After a short break, students filtered back into the room. Jen asked that they do what she would have asked any composition class to do on the first day: form a circle. They froze and resisted movement that would create a more conversational group that encouraged face-to-face interaction and accountability. "No really, I'm from English," Jennifer joked. "I like circles." Elizabeth immediately stepped in and stated, "She said form a circle. So do it. Move." Her direct approach, as opposed to Jen's indirect one, got results. It was the first of many lessons that Jen would have to confront. In her past composition classes, her uneasy but unyielding desire to come out to students as queer manifested when she described her research interests and family as part of her changing perspective as a writer, as a resident in western Massachusetts, and as a person who embraced the access granted by the Gay Marriage Act. The Gay Marriage Act, passed in Massachusetts in 2005, amid huge controversy and protest, granted queer and same-sex partners the right to marry, and as a legal issue, was obviously relevant in a CJ class where theories of equality and social justice were central. In addition, writing classes, especially as taught by Jen, often call upon or bring into sharp relief our identities and families.

The different methods of instruction (reflected in part by the material traditionally covered in each class, the different outcomes our department curricula required, the different ethos of each discipline, and our (un)willingness to impose or make manifest our identities as instructors and people outside of the classroom) represented a split that was evident to students and instructors alike. At the same time, we think students were, in "The Writer and the Detective" course, actually uniting both parts of campus, the isolated heteronormative CJ department with its over-determined vocational focus and the main campus with its liberal arts core curriculum emphasis. Furthermore, many of the students were happy to celebrate the CJ system as one that punished un-problematized, dyed-in-the-wool wrong-doers or even sometimes "came down too hard on high school students who just want to have a good time." The first time we taught the class, there was a vast gap between the material presented in the CJ textbook and the lives of those who exist in an unequal power structure.

A Linked Course

Our efforts to implement integrated courses throughout our school began four years ago, when we received an internal grant meant to provide faculty members with opportunities to try out new pedagogical initiatives. As a way to challenge student resistance to a liberal arts curriculum, we co-taught an integrated learning community that met back to back and combined the content of Theories of Crime (Criminal Justice 121) with Freshman Composition II (English 102). Perhaps due in part to our status as junior faculty, we took on the linked part of the course as an addition to our normal 4–4 teaching load. In essence, we each taught a fifth class. Unlike the second time we taught the course under the auspices of the grant, at first we didn't receive any institutional credit or monetary reimbursement of the additional work required.

In our integrated class, we encouraged 21 CJ students to simultaneously take the second of two required composition courses and Theories of Crime, a course required of all CJ majors to approach writing and CJ as both "writers" and "detectives." Our hope was to sharpen students' skills in story-telling, observation, and critical thinking. The obvious homophobia, racism, and ignorance of cultural difference that emerged the first time we taught the course drove our desire to alter our pedagogical understandings of our own disciplines and influenced both of our approaches to teaching.

This experience drove our desire to enact an intersectional analysis of the oppression and white privilege that shaped classroom interactions and assumptions.

An Intersectional Approach

The second time we taught the course, we used an intersectional model to better incorporate a means to challenge students' ignorance, homophobia,

NEW DIRECTIONS FOR TEACHING AND LEARNING • DOI: 10.1002/tl

and racism by more clearly accounting for issues of power, gender, and sexuality. Our grant, the "Pilot Program to Encourage Co-Taught Community Courses," proposed to create learning communities across disciplines that had the following structure: each learning community was co-designed and taught by two faculty members whose courses met back-to-back. To accommodate the time and effort required to create learning communities and to receive institutional credit for time spent in what amounted to an additional class, each person who taught a learning community received one course reassignment. We also received training and suggestions from two instructors at a neighboring college: Holyoke Community College. The most important challenge they issued was to help us move our courses beyond a "linkage" of two separate disciplines to one "integrated" course. The differences between a course that is linked and a course that is integrated is something we worked on when we taught the course a second time.

What Changed?

By revising our pedagogical approach to the course a year later, it was clear to us that writing was the means by which these two courses could integrate. Therefore, as opposed to reinforcing stereotypes students brought to the course, while doing the hard work of encouraging students to write composition papers that integrated CJ concepts, we needed to encourage students through writing to more directly question the authority they are encouraged to assume as CJ majors and students with white privilege. Throughout our teaching of the course and our subsequent revision of it, we found that composition courses and writing activities we ask students to do shapes and establishes a framework for the interdisciplinary nature of the course and therefore lends itself to an intersectional analysis approach.

This time, supported by an internal grant sponsored by Academic Affairs, we worked to make our courses "integrated" as opposed to "linked." Specifically, we worked hard to problematize concepts of "authority," "discretion," and "power" as pieces of identity and culture. In preparation for this integration, we attended a workshop offered by two instructors from a neighboring college and were encouraged to create a "theme," which we could use as a way to create a bridge between the two disciplines. We also revised the writing assignments and the multiple-choice tests students needed to take to ensure they knew the vocabulary for CJ, and worked to make explicit and implicit connections between the content in each of our disciplines so that students recognized how the content of one discipline can enhance their understandings of the content and the ethos of another discipline.

The writing assignments we initially designed for the course when we first taught it used language that allowed students to rely only upon their personal experiences, and in the absence of another structure to help them understand issues of power and to write about them, they relied upon the language and ethos readily available to them in the CJ program. There was little opportunity for them to rethink the assumptions they had about power and authority because the assignments didn't explicitly require them to do so. In "Reading and Writing Differences: The Problematic of Experience," feminist compositionist Min-Zhan Lu (1998) argues that those who both occupy privileged spaces and invoke experience as evidence need to examine the ways that privilege may have shaped their personal experiences. She claims that "feminist readers need to reflect on their privileged social location and be vigilant toward the tendency to invoke experience as an inherent right that erases differences along lines of race, class, gender, or sexual identity" (p. 436). Although some of the language in the first assignment may have attempted to encourage students to perform that sort of analysis, because she believes that the students brought so many unexamined assumptions, the structure of her writing assignments meant that the students not only tended to assume an erasure along the lines of race, class, gender, and sexual identity, but often openly denigrated that which was not white, middle-class, heterosexual, and in accordance with stringent gender norms and roles.

We wanted the students who took the course to have a better and more empathetic approach to the people they were hoping to "protect and serve" and to be able to communicate better with that population. As a result of the different disciplinary conventions or types of academic discourse reflected in the two disciplines, our revised class had a structure for addressing homophobia, racism, and misogyny using conflict theory. We addressed such questions as "Who has the power to write the laws? What are the politics of excluding representatives from different races, classes, ethnicities, religions, and genders from power?" We came to see that the tools for studying and critiquing power can be accessed within CJ when writing is applied and students are encouraged to struggle with the profound implications of their actions within our Western system. In theories such as conflict theory, which assumes different interest groups and political agendas, and restorative justice, which also argues that we can have a less incarceration- and punishment-focused CJ system, writing can be a link to students' cognitive and social development in the classroom. When taught using a rhetorical model, writing encourages students to make choices according to the audience they hope to engage, a process similar to the ethical decision making inherent in CJ and law enforcement work.

Because our teaching the second time focused more directly on identity and challenged students' assumptions more openly, the ethos of the class was more openly resistant the second time around. However, because identity issues were clearly articulated and discussed (as opposed to recognized but unacknowledged), the debates, discussion, and subsequent writing were more confrontational. Ironically, they were also more clearly thought out and critical. Overall, it seemed that the students were more engaged and invested.

Lu (1998) argues that "Experience should motivate us to care about another's differences and should disrupt the material conditions that give rise to it" (p. 436). As a way to facilitate critical thinking about themselves as people who will have real power over a population comprised of disenfranchised, non-white, and often impoverished people, we revised the writing assignments to encourage the students in the course to more directly examine structures of power, something that is enabled by the concepts introduced in the Theories of Crime course. As was reinforced for us both, it isn't a natural tendency for the students in the CJ program (maybe in any program) to enact that sort of disruption primarily because their desire to belong to it makes them far too invested in it. We believe that the revised assignments allowed the students the opportunity to think more critically about how they understood power and hoped to use it, and that they helped a population of students often resistant to writing and what they deem "academic bullshit," but what we might call "critical inquiry." Why, for example, are the poorest Americans on Death Row?

Still, the desire of students to maintain a separation between the English part of the course and the CJ part of the course remained. Although we struggled (in the planning of assignments, activities, in our choices of books, and sometimes while we were teaching) to create this integration, we were also attempting to learn the language and norms of another discipline. One example helped to show that students had observed our ongoing work at integration. In a one-on-one writing conference, Bobby asked Jen "Are you really taking notes when she [Elizabeth] lectures? Or, are you just writing?" Surprised, she assured him she really was, and that she, like him, was new to concepts like "rational choice theory" and to CJ theorists like Cesare Lombroso. Elizabeth was surprised by how powerful *A Jury of Her Peers* by Susan Glaspell ([1917] 2007) was as a teaching tool to show students that all the facts of a case could be hidden from a detective due to social, cultural, and gender norms. Students and instructors were surprised at how the hard work of learning to think differently and write more critically came into sharp relief in this integrated class. The two disciplines could truly complement each other.

Conclusion

Elizabeth believes that she has only benefited from getting back to her roots as a social science professor who tries to use writing and ethnographic observation as a way to reach every student's interest in every topic and every theory introduced in the Theories of Crime course. Students readily understand and are engaged by the human drama of crime, but do not often get to understand their own biases and the social implications of

New Directions for Teaching and Learning • DOI: 10.1002/tl

these biases as part of the social tragedies they are immersed in. Drawing from Caleb Carr's *The Alienist* (1995) and the disturbing portrait of psychopathy in the film *Capote* (2006), students wrote to better understand the details of these cases, the array of possible emotions and motives for crime, and the theories that underpin the action of the offenders. Writing engages the CJ students' selves, makes for more critical and astute observations and insights into what they might easily miss due to their particular race, class, gender, ethnicity, or sexual orientation. Students, as consumers of crime narratives, seem hungry for redemptive stories (if not enactments of legal punishment based on clear understandings of good and evil), but more importantly, these types of texts allow them deeper insight into their own biases. Students were able to recognize how good and evil are far more ambiguous and complex in actual human drama. To teach these topics and theories without the insights into self-study writing can bring would make for a narrative that cannot begin to be resolved, a social warning about crime but not much insight into the social costs.

Our work with the linked and integrated courses has made four points very clear to Jen. (1) Students are not entirely wrong in their perception that there are huge differences in the ethos between two disciplines. Her own struggle to learn some of the vocabulary of CJ and integrate it with the composition course she usually teaches has made her more empathetic to students' struggles to apply what they learn in composition to the writing they do in other courses. In fact, when polling students, we found that many were initially driven to take the integrated course because they thought it would "make English less boring and more relevant." (2) Integrated courses like ours (as opposed to "linked" courses) can go far in helping students (and instructors) to see the ways the writing process and skills often taught in composition are transferable to other disciplines, but it requires that we, the instructors in both the "different" disciplines and in composition courses, essentially position ourselves as we ask our students to do: as strangers. (3) As composition instructors, we need to understand that because the disciplines are more different than we might like to acknowledge, the course and the knowledge that results from the "integration" is, like the writing/language of each discipline itself, somewhat specific. In other words, linking composition with Women's Studies or with Movement Science will probably yield different insights. (4) The role of administration in supporting and underwriting these endeavors by financing them through specific material practices such as course reassignment credits enables the sort of collaboration such endeavors require. Such support is an investment in both student and instructor development, and acknowledges that in an economy/world that increasingly values interdisciplinary approaches and the thinking that results from such endeavors, administration must support and facilitate that type of dynamic learning.

Together, we ultimately argue for the transformative nature of institutionally supported interdisciplinary approaches (which make possible linked and integrated courses) which enable instructor reflection on and change to pedagogical norms and personal values and reinforce the rhetorical, reflective, and transactive purposes of writing and learning in a liberal arts institution.

References

Brooks, R., and Stassinos, E. "Lesbian and Gay Topics in Criminal Justice Textbooks." Paper presented at the 2006 Academy of Criminal Justice Sciences Annual Meetings, Baltimore, Md., March 2006.

Capote. Directed by Bennett Miller. Culver City, Calif.: Sony Pictures, 2006, Video DVD.

Carr, C. *The Alienist.* London: Warner Books, 1995.

Eubanks, P., and Schaeffer, J. D. "A Kind Word for Bullshit: The Problem of Academic Writing." *College Composition and Communication,* 2008, *59,* 372–388.

Glaspell, S. "A Jury of Her Peers." In A. Charters and S. Charters (eds.), *Literature and Its Writers.* (4th ed.) Bedford, N.Y.: St. Marten's, 2007. (Originally published 1917)

Herrington, A., and Curtis, M. (2000). *Persons in Process: Four Stories of Writing and Personal Development in College.* Urbana, IL: National Council of Teachers of English.

Lu, M.-Z. "Reading and Writing Difference: The Problematic of Experience." *Feminism and Composition Studies:* In S.C. Jarratt and L. Worsham (eds.), *Other Words.* New York: MLA, 1998.

Siegel, L. *Criminology: Theories, Patterns, and Typologies.* (9th ed.) Belmont, Calif.: Thomson-Wadsworth, 2007.

Wise, D. *Nightmover: How Aldrich Ames Sold the CIA to the KGB for $4.6 Million.* New York: Harper-Collins, 1995.

Wise, D. *Spy: The Inside Story of How the FBI's Robert Hanssen Betrayed America.* New York: Random House, 2003.

Jennifer DiGrazia is assistant professor of English, Westfield State University.

Elizabeth Stassinos is associate professor of criminal justice, Westfield State University.

New Directions for Teaching and Learning • DOI: 10.1002/tl

The authors use a case study and the theory of intersectionality to expand strategies for collaborative teaching.

Using an Intersectional Approach to Deepen Collaborative Teaching

Susan M. Pliner, Jonathan Iuzzini, Cerri A. Banks

Scholars who study teaching and learning have provided the academy with a range of progressive pedagogies that move beyond traditional ways of teaching. In the call for the use of diverse classroom practices in higher education many have highlighted the benefits and challenges that come with collaborative teaching models (Lester and Evans, 2009; Ouellett and Fraser, 2005). Collaborative teaching is seen as beneficial for the following reasons:

1. Collaborative teaching enhances faculty members' development as teachers, provides opportunities for them to articulate their thinking about pedagogical decision-making, and provides support when discussing difficult topics in the classroom.
2. Collaborative teaching has a positive impact on faculty members' relationships with students as it enables faculty to assess a wider range of student abilities.
3. Collaborative teaching broadens students' understanding of course content because it pushes students to engage with the range of perspectives found in any academic community.
4. Collaborative teaching provides specific academic skill sets as it encourages students to develop critical analytical skills and learn to communicate across difference.

In this chapter we examine collaborative teaching through an intersectional lens. Intersectionality as a theoretical concept has practical

NEW DIRECTIONS FOR TEACHING AND LEARNING, no. 125, Spring 2011 © Wiley Periodicals, Inc.
Published online in Wiley Online Library (wileyonlinelibrary.com) • DOI: 10.1002/tl.432

implications for the ways faculty understand and practice skills related to teaching and for the ways students learn (Banks, Iuzzini, and Pliner, 2010). Through the use of a case study, we discuss how an intersectional lens enriches collaboration by facilitating a classroom community where a diverse range of identities and perspectives are utilized in learning processes. This conceptual lens provides ways for faculty to deliver content knowledge and to simultaneously create and sustain inclusive and authentic classrooms.

Collaborative Teaching and Intersectionality

Collaborative teaching can take many forms (for in-depth reviews, see Ouellett and Fraser, 2005; Vogler and Long, 2004). Dugan and Letterman (2008) suggest that although students see the value in courses that are taught collaboratively they may experience frustrations when there are communication and organizational breakdowns between the collaborating faculty members. Past research has examined how collaborating faculty members can be trained to maximize their work together. For example, Eby (2001) suggested that there are "two necessary and complementary steps for interdisciplinary teaching and learning": "developing disciplinary self-awareness" and "becoming a learner" (p. 29, cited by Stevenson, Duran, Barrett, and Colarulli, 2005, p. 27).

We suggest that the concept of intersectionality requires three additional components as being essential in collaborative teaching: (1) an awareness and understanding of self in relation to socially constructed identities, (2) an awareness and understanding of self in relation to a collaborator's socially constructed identities, and (3) a shared awareness and understanding developed by collaborating faculty of the potential impact of their identities and their students' identities on the processes of teaching and learning. Each of these components must be considered in synergy with one another and in relation to historical and social contexts. For our purposes, we discuss the first two components together. The following analysis of our case study will illustrate this synergistic approach.

Hobart and William Smith Colleges (HWS; Geneva, New York) comprise a small, coordinate, private, residential liberal arts institution with approximately 2,000 undergraduate students. With 195 faculty members, the institution has an 11 to 1 faculty-student ratio. Approximately 18 percent of the campus community identifies as faculty of color and 14 percent identifies as students of color. In the past five years, the institution has demonstrated a commitment towards issues of diversity with the development of a Presidential Commission on Inclusive Excellence. Beyond the Commission, the institution supports inclusive teaching through the Center for Teaching and Learning, which Pliner directs as the Associate Dean for Teaching, Learning, and Assessment.

NEW DIRECTIONS FOR TEACHING AND LEARNING • DOI: 10.1002/tl

Our working relationship began when the three of us were appointed to serve on the Commission in early 2007. Banks and Pliner (Education professors) and Iuzzini (Psychology professor) all take an intersectional approach to teaching and scholarship within their disciplines and are known on campus for their commitment to social justice in and out of the classroom.

In the fall 2008 semester, Banks and Iuzzini, supported by Pliner, collaboratively taught an interdisciplinary course entitled "Intersections of Race, Class, and Gender in Everyday Life." As Banks and Iuzzini worked through the challenges of team-teaching for the first time, they were empowered by our institution's commitment to this work in two ways: (1) the director of the Center for Teaching and Learning (Pliner) supports faculty development, and (2) she serves in this role with an expertise in social justice education. At HWS, collaborative teaching across disciplines is encouraged through our institution's bi-disciplinary program. One of the most important ways the institution supports this work is by granting each faculty member a full course credit for co-teaching the course. In our case, both instructors planned, prepared, and were present for every class meeting.

In the Education department, Banks had been offering courses on multicultural education and other social justice issues. In the Psychology department, Iuzzini had been teaching a seminar on the social psychology of prejudice and intergroup relations. All of these courses were geared to advanced students, so to reach a wider range of students we decided that this co-taught course would be open to students at any level and there would be no prerequisites.

There were 36 students enrolled, representing a range of majors, class years, and levels of expertise with the course content. The course content lent itself to students considering their socially constructed identities in a number of ways. Thirteen identified as students of color, thirty identified as women, and there was a broad range of social class identities. No students openly identified as gay, lesbian, bisexual, or transgendered. Eight self-identified as having a learning disability and six identified as having psychological disabilities.

Developing an Understanding of Self in Relation to One's Social Identities and to a Collaborator's Social Identities. Identities, like race, class, gender, and sexuality, are socially constructed; that is, they are defined and bound by inequitable power structures grounded in historical and current social contexts (Banks, 2009). The process of understanding self in relation to one's identities and as an educator may occur as a natural evolution of self-reflection in the teaching role (Weinstein and Obear, 1992). Regardless of how much or little of this evolution has occurred, the process of working with a collaborator—communicating, reflecting, and analyzing—in a team teaching situation should deepen each individual's awareness of how social identities impact educational spaces and the

New Directions for Teaching and Learning • DOI: 10.1002/tl

collaboration. Even when people share identity characteristics there are variances based on geography, history, and experiential knowledge (Bell, Love, Washington, and Weinstein, 2007). These contexts inform how we understand and interact with one another and within institutions like education, which reinforce inequitable structures. It is critical that each collaborator recognize when socially constructed ideas (e.g., stereotypes, privilege) are infiltrating collaborative thought processes and actions and creating barriers. This realization facilitates collaborative classrooms that challenge and interrupt social inequity.

When preparing to teach a course, collaborators applying an intersectional lens should develop knowledge of themselves and their social identities in relationship to teaching and learning. They must also develop an understanding of each other's social identities and perspectives and those of their students because this understanding will inform what happens in the classroom. In collaboration, we are not "neutral," "disconnected" participants. Intersectionality teaches us that our identities and the power structures in which they are embedded are always a part of teaching and learning processes.

Case Study. Applying an intersectional approach to our course preparation to Banks and Iuzzini meant going beyond content construction to addressing issues of our identities. We began with a consultation with Pliner in which we developed a shared foundation about collaborative teaching. This conversation prompted us to consider our socially constructed identities while preparing to collaborate. Banks, an African American woman from a working class family, and Iuzzini, a Jewish Italian man from an upper middle class family, both identify as heterosexual. We knew that the difference in race and gender would be the most immediate and visible way identity would be infused into the classroom dynamic. Our initial discussions covered why we had chosen our respective professional paths and our learning experiences as college students. Most importantly, we shared autobiographies, remembering and recounting times when we faced prejudice and discrimination and honestly acknowledging times when we used our privilege. We discussed learning about the larger historical and social implications of identity and how we had integrated this academic knowledge with our personal experiences to create a foundation for our teaching philosophy and classroom practice. This enabled each of us, as we prepared our syllabus and chose texts, to get a sense of the other's expectations in the classroom and of our respective strengths and weaknesses.

An intersectional perspective necessitates attention to issues of identity, power, and privilege in collaborative teaching relationships. This lens recognizes that styles of interaction are often cultural and social and related to features of identity like race, class, sexuality, and gender. In Pliner's work as a faculty developer conducting classroom observations and consultations, she has found that male faculty are often more readily respected than female faculty as experts in their fields. Women can find that students challenge their expertise by expressing skepticism about their ideas. They report that students stereotypically expect them to be more nurturing and flexible with attendance, participation, and assessment.

Women of color face these challenges in multiplicative ways because the socially constructed ideas about their race and gender make them even less likely to be respected (Brewer, 1999; Collins, 1993). Students are often surprised to see that the woman of color in the room is the instructor. Once the realization sets in, students express skepticism about their motives for teaching, their knowledge, and the validity of their degrees. We know from much research on attitudes toward affirmative action that in the absence of concrete information, people assume that members of marginalized groups (especially women and people of color) must be less qualified for whatever job they intend to perform (Heilman and Blader, 2001). This type of inter-sectional consideration demonstrates the necessity to expand conversations about interaction styles when co-teaching to include a social and cultural analysis.

Banks and Iuzzini recognized that interactive styles can be connected to identity and that teaching in collaboration is, in part, about the relation-ship between the two instructors. Specifically, in this case, the first thing students would see is a white man and a black woman. We understood that stereotypes could infiltrate the classroom environment based on our identi-ties and the students' identities. There was potential for students in the course to assume that a white male faculty member (Iuzzini) would not have sufficient personal experience or expertise to teach the course mate-rial and thus dismiss his contributions (Ouellett and Fraser, 2005). Many students in the class recognized Banks and Iuzzini as having expertise in diversity work, and so it was imperative that we worked to challenge these stereotypes that could occur in our classroom. Our efforts to challenge these stereotypes involved being conscious of the back-and-forth dynamic of our co-lecturing. We leveraged our differing disciplinary backgrounds and took turns presenting new or difficult content. We asked each other for clarification, we modeled respectful disagreement, and used academic scholarship from experts representing a range of social identities. This pro-vided our students with a model of collaboration that validated each instructor's expertise; each of us was seen as a knowledgeable and valuable contributor.

Applying an intersectional approach gave us a lens through which we could better understand each other as co-teachers, enhance our patterns of communication and organization, and disrupt traditional patterns of power and privilege in the classroom.

Understanding the Potential Impact of Faculty Identities and Their Students' Identities on the Processes of Teaching and Learning. Classroom dynamics are impacted by students' identity-based lived experiences (Fox, 2001; Tatum, 1997). Collaborating professors must know who is or is not in the classroom (Adams, Jones, and Tatum, 2007). An intersectional approach deepens that consideration to include how the coming together of the identities represented in the classroom, the impact of limited representation (e.g., being the only Native American student in the room), and the impact of excluded or invisible identity markers (e.g., being gay or having a learning disability) can impact the goals we have set out for any learning activity. This requires modeling for students on how to reflect on and communicate information related to identity.

Case Study. To get to know their students, the first learning activity Banks and Iuzzini assigned asked students to write a brief autobiography about their identity and one or two significant experiences they had with difference. Prior to giving this assignment, Banks and Iuzzini shared their autobiographies with each other and with the class so that they could develop an understanding of (1) what we meant by identity, (2) what an experience with difference could include, and (3) the kind of language they could use to communicate these ideas. In addition, we wanted them to experience an intersectional analysis even before we introduced the concept. To that end, in his autobiography Iuzzini wrote about growing up Jewish with an Italian last name, in a neighborhood and in schools with very few Jewish peers. He described his experience as an adolescent witnessing anti-Semitic remarks and behaviors but maintaining a level of detachment from the experience by hiding behind his last name. Banks discussed her conflicted relationship with social class because she now exists at a level of class different from what she grew up in and different from many of her family members. She explained how existing at a more privileged level of social class did not protect her from race and gender bias. Both included a discussion of how our prior experiences motivated us to develop an understanding of social justice and how this philosophy is the foundation of our collaborative teaching.

The student autobiographies were useful in a number of ways as we strategized weekly about how to address students' different levels of familiarity and comfort with course material. First, we used the autobiographies to scaffold learning activities and assigned student work. For example, we used information in the autobiographies to assign students into groups for in-class fishbowl discussions of assigned readings, ensuring that each group was diverse in terms of social identities and in terms of expertise with course material. Second, the autobiographies informed the individualized approach we took as we met with students during their preparation for the course's major writing assignments (e.g., critical reflection paper, policy brief paper, literature review paper). Our students' range of personal experiences and academic expertise meant that they approached these assignments with varied levels of apprehension connected to their understanding of course content. By relying on information from the autobiographies we were prepared to guide students through the challenges associated with each assignment, thus providing a significant learning experience for each student. Third, the autobiographies helped us to understand why our students had vastly different levels of confidence about engaging in class discussions on difficult topics. Students who had less prior experience with diversity were concerned that they would say the wrong thing and offend others in class. At the same time, students with background in these issues grew impatient with their peers who had less preparation. The most frustrating moments for everyone in the room occurred when students who were uninformed were very vocal.

Banks and Iuzzini recognized that these dynamics were a result of our collaborative decision to not require prerequisites, but because we had each student's autobiography we were able to understand them at a level that went beyond what we saw on the surface. For example, one woman had a habit of blurting out comments that indicated that she was not applying the theoretical concepts to the conversations we were having about difference. In her autobiography, and in a conversation with us, she discussed her struggles with her bi-racial identity (having a black parent and a white parent) and assumptions about whiteness and social class. Although we too had discussed our frustrations about this student during our preparation sessions, unlike her classmates, we had the benefit of understanding how this struggle impacted her learning and class behavior. We knew that at her core this student wanted to understand the content to make sense of her own experiences. This allowed us to discuss the impact her behavior was having on the class and facilitate less frustrating ways for her to participate. We met with her on several occasions to discuss her class participation and coached her on using effective strategies for contributing to discussions. We advised her to formulate her thoughts and prepare her comments in advance. Over time, the student utilized these strategies and made more meaningful contributions to class discussions. Through their collaborative process, Banks was able to reflect upon the intersections of race, class, and gender and their impact on learning, while Iuzzini listened and utilized this information in his own thinking about and interactions with this student.

Our awareness of (and our communication with each other about) our own identities (both in historical terms and in relation to our current social context) made it important for us to engage in an ongoing dialogue. This dialogue impacted our approach to how we prepared for class meetings and the nature of our lectures and discussions, and most importantly, influenced how we were able to manage classroom dynamics and model appropriate interventions and flexibility for our students. We created classroom activities that would make the intersections of identity and power visible and assist students with taking on multiple perspectives while learning course content and interacting with faculty and peers.

Conclusion

Through a discussion of intersectionality in theoretical terms and in the context of our case study we have suggested that applying an intersectional lens can enhance collaborative teaching, and we learned several lessons. For example, as mentioned, our course had no prerequisites. As a result, we expended time and energy on issues that may not have developed among students with more similar academic standing. In the future we will offer this as either an introductory course or an advanced course with appropriate prerequisites.

In our case study we emphasized the ways the autobiography assignment positively impacted our collaborative teaching experience. Upon reflection while writing this article, Pliner pushed Banks and Iuzzini to consider how the autobiography could have been used even more effectively. We could have had our students share their autobiographies with each other. This could have further strengthened our classroom community, reduced some of the frustration we witnessed during discussions, and provided a richer intersectional layer to examine socially constructed identities.

Lester and Evans (2009) suggest that "when we are willing to engage in reflective practice with those around us, listen to the thoughts and perspectives of others, even when there is inherent risk of conflict and disagreement, the opportunity to build greater understanding emerges . . . we make space to *build something bigger* than we could have built ourselves" (pp. 380–381).

Collaborative teaching with an intersectional lens is always strengthened when it is endorsed and supported by institutional structures. This includes curricular initiatives that promote collaborative teaching, training for faculty through centers for teaching and learning, and incentives for faculty to participate.

There is value to building a community of teacher–scholars who can recognize multiple perspectives and analyze content within historical and social contexts in every discipline. When we teach collaboratively using an intersectional lens in preparation, execution, and reflection, we expand the potential for authentic student learning.

References

Adams, M., Jones, J., and Tatum, B. D. (2007). "Knowing Our Students." In M. Adams, L. A. Bell, and P. Griffin (eds.), *Teaching for Diversity and Social Justice.* (2nd ed.) New York: Routledge, 2007.

Banks, C. A. *Black Women Undergraduates, Cultural Capital, and College Success.* New York: Peter Lang Publishing, 2009.

Banks, C. A., Iuzzini, J., and Pliner, S. M. "Intersecting Identities and the Work of Faculty Development." In J. Miller (ed.), *To Improve the Academy: Resources for Faculty, Instructional, and Organizational Development*, 2010, 29, 132–144.

Bell, L. A., Love, B. J., Washington, S., and Weinstein, G. "Knowing Ourselves as Social Justice Educators." In M. Adams, L. A. Bell, and P. Griffin (eds.), *Teaching for Diversity and Social Justice*. (2nd ed.) New York: Routledge, 2007.

Brewer, R. M. "Theorizing Race, Class, and Gender: The New Scholarship of Black Feminist Intellectuals and Black Women's Labor." *Race, Class, and Gender,* 1999, 6(2), 29–47.

Collins, P. H. "Toward a New Vision: Race, Class, and Gender as Categories of Analysis and Connection." *Race, Class, and Gender*, 1993, 1, 25–45.

Dugan, K., and Letterman, M. "Student Appraisals of Collaborative Teaching." *College Teaching*, 2008, 56, 11–15.

Eby, K. K. "Teaching and Learning from an Interdisciplinary Perspective." *Peer Review*, 2001, 3(4), 28–33.

Fox, H. *When Race Breaks Out: Conversations About Racism in College Classrooms*. New York: Peter Lang Publishing, 2001.

Heilman, M. E., and Blader, S. L. "Assuming Preferential Selection When the Admissions Policy is Unknown: The Effects of Gender Rarity." *Journal of Applied Psychology*, 2001, 86, 188–193.

Lester, J. N., and Evans, K. R. "Instructors' Experiences of Collaboratively Teaching: Building Something Bigger." *International Journal of Teaching and Learning in Higher Education*, 2009, 20, 373–382.

Ouellett, M. L., and Fraser, E. C. "Teaching Together: Interracial Teams." In M. L. Ouellett (ed.), *Teaching Inclusively: Resources for Course, Department and Institutional Change in Higher Education*. Stillwater, OK: New Forums Press, 2005.

Stevenson, C. B., Duran, R. L., Barrett, K. A., and Colarulli, G. C. "Fostering Faculty Collaboration in Learning Communities: A Developmental Approach." *Innovative Higher Education*, 2005, 30, 23–36.

Tatum, B. D. *Why Are All the Black Kids Sitting Together in the Cafeteria? And Other Conversations About Race: A Psychologist Explains the Development of Racial Identity*. New York: Basic Books, 1997.

Vogler, K. E., and Long, E. "Team Teaching Two Sections of the Same Undergraduate Course: A Case Study." *College Teaching*, 2004, 51(4), 122–126.

Weinstein, G., and Obear, K. "Bias Issues in the Classroom: Encounters With the Teaching Self." In M. Adams (ed.), *Promoting Diversity in College Classrooms: Innovative Responses for the Curriculum, Faculty, and Institutions*. New Directions for Teaching and Learning, no. 52. San Francisco: Jossey-Bass, 1992.

SUSAN M. PLINER *is associate dean for teaching, learning, and assessment, director of the Centennial Center for Leadership, and an assistant professor of education at Hobart & William Smith Colleges.*

JONATHAN IUZZINI *is an assistant professor of psychology and an affiliate of the interdisciplinary program in public policy studies at Hobart & William Smith Colleges.*

CERRI A. BANKS *is dean of William Smith College and an assistant professor of education at Hobart & William Smith Colleges.*

SECTION THREE

Points of Interface

5

The author describes how a pedagogical approach utilizing insights and principles from queer theory facilitated an intersectional analysis in a large lecture, general education course on "Gender, Sexuality, Literature and Culture" at the University of Massachusetts Amherst.

The Intersectional Potential of Queer Theory: An Example from a General Education Course in English

Deborah Carlin

In the fall of 2006 the English department at the University of Massachusetts tasked me with creating a general education lecture course that would serve three hundred students, many of them non-English majors for whom this might be the only literature course they would take in their college career. The previous incarnation of this course was a thirty-five student lecture/discussion format taught by graduate student instructors and entitled "Man and Woman in Literature." Renamed the broader, less binary, and more inclusive "Gender, Sexuality, Literature and Culture," this course was mandated by the university to meet a global and cultural diversity requirement. Such courses are designed to emphasize how norms and values differ across societies and are to be informed by pluralistic perspectives of Western, African, Asian, Latin American, Middle Eastern, and Asian cultures. Demographically, 82 percent of students enrolled in the course to fulfill a general education requirement, and 79 percent of all students were registered as freshmen (56 percent) and sophomores (23 percent). Given the university's specific directive to investigate and analyze norms and values and its emphasis on encouraging pluralistic perspectives, I decided to adopt a queerly informed pedagogical approach to the material rather than one that relied on identity-based categories of gender (man, woman) and of sexuality (heterosexual, homosexual, bisexual). My goal was to use queer theory's deconstructive methodology to disrupt and destabilize potentially

New Directions for Teaching and Learning, no. 125, Spring 2011 © Wiley Periodicals, Inc.
Published online in Wiley Online Library (wileyonlinelibrary.com) • DOI: 10.1002/tl.433

predetermined student conceptions of gender and sexuality in ways that fostered intersectional analysis because "sexuality is always already intersecting with other vectors of identity and difference" (Lovass, Elia, and Yep, 2006, p. 12).

Queer Theory and Intersectional Analysis

Although the specific historical evolution of Lesbian, Gay, Bisexual, and Transgender (LGBT) Studies and queer theory since the 1970s that Seidman (1995) provides is beyond the scope of this article, a working definition of queer theory, articulated cogently by Jagose (1996), posits that "queer defines those gestures or analytical models which dramatise incoherencies in the allegedly stable relations between chromosomal sex, gender and sexual desire. Resisting that model of stability—which claims heterosexuality as its origin, when it is more properly its effect—queer focuses on mismatches between sex, gender and desire" (p. 3).

The term "queer" is frequently misunderstood to function as either a noun or as an identity category; however, it should more accurately be deployed as a verb (to queer), one that signifies action rather than individuals. If "queer" can be said to occupy any stable location, it might best be conceived as "an interrogative and, frequently, interventionist position, taken on the basis of a skepticism toward the supposedly 'natural' undergirdings of human society such as sexuality, race, class, and gender" (Holmes, 1994). As the late Eve Sedgwick, one of the pioneers of queer theory, reminded us, the "word 'queer' itself means across—it comes from the Indo-European root –twerkw, which also yields the German quer (traverse), Latin torquere (to twist), English athwart" (1993, p. xii). As a methodology that refutes and refuses the safe stability of specific sexual and gendered identity formations, queer theory invites intersectional analyses because it "privileges difference rather than essence in the construction of identity" and insists that "who we are depends more on our relations to the others around us than on any innate characteristics" (Berlant, 1994). Looking beyond sex and gender alone, across multiple, intersecting, and interdependent axes of self construction (nationality, race, ethnicity, class, religion, abilities, geography, and historical era), queer theory inherently rejects, as Slagle (2006) argues, "any approaches to the construction of identities from a universal perspective" (p. 318). Because its impetus is the deconstruction of fixed identities and the dismantling of hierarchies, queer theory is both an appropriate and constructive tool in any intersectional analysis that examines how multiple and interconnected strands of social categories and power relations shape human experience and create systemic oppressions. Both queer theory and intersectional analyses then are linked by their investment "in a world in which particular differences (we all have them) are not inherently valued over other differences" (Slagle, 2006, p. 318). Indeed, identifying the mutual concerns of queer theory and intersectional analysis calls into question the complaint of some critics that deconstruction is somehow synonymous with an apolitical stance and that, as a result, queer theory has no political agenda or effects in the material world; Kirsch's (2000) critique that "it is certainly safer to *deconstruct* theories of social being than to *construct* modes of social action" (p. 31) must, I would argue, be tempered and perhaps even reevaluated in the light of Hall's (1997) assertion that "Queer tacticians do not imagine that they will destroy the system nor do they deny its existence, but instead, they provoke it, call its bluff, nudge it towards self-interrogation and change" (p. 5). Rather than retreating into the academic and apolitical— terms that are all too often conflated—queer interrogations resolutely position themselves in the realm of the political in their examination of how social relationships, including those located in sexuality and in gender, always, *a priori*, involve power and authority.

Structure of the Course

Because large lecture courses inherently create distance between the instructor and students, and even among students themselves, I designed aspects of the course to foster a greater dialogue between both myself and the students during our two lectures per week, and among the students in their specific discussion sections (containing thirty students and taught once a week by graduate instructors). In lectures, I incorporated PRS (Personal Response System) questions into each class; these questions were open-ended and interpretive in nature and enabled me to venture into the auditorium with a portable microphone to allow students to elaborate on their chosen answers. For example, in a discussion of Nigerian writer, Chris Abani's novel *Graceland* (2004), I asked the students the following question which appeared on a large screen at the front of the auditorium: "I think that the most influential male figure on Elvis' journey into manhood is (1. Innocent 2. Sunday 3. Redemption 4. The King of Beggars 5. Okun) because . . ." Students selected their answer on their remote device and the PRS software tallied all their choices and produced a graph showing the breakdown of the responses. It was at this juncture that I would make my way into the audience where students (usually between four and six) were encouraged to articulate their interpretations, to explain, in short, why they thought what they did and what evidence in the text inclined them toward a particular choice. My intent in this process was not only to foster a more cohesive feeling among this very large group, but to incorporate student ideas into the lecture space to counter my own singular authority as the instructor and primary voice in the room.

The attempt to ameliorate the anonymity of a large lecture course and to increase student investment in their own voices also extended into the structure of how student writing was integrated into the course. Given that 79 percent of students in the course were freshmen or sophomores and thus less accustomed to writing longer, analytical essays about literature, it seemed far more efficacious and pedagogically sound to require students to submit weekly, short (1–2 paragraph) responses to questions posed on the course's WebCT site rather than two longer (5–7 page) essays. Questions were posted each weekend. (Example: "In your response last week, you discussed a gender norm that you witnessed or experienced. How does the structure of the society in *The Shore of Women* present a reversal of our norms? Are there any moments in the novel that reflect the present reality of our American life? Using specific examples from the novel, discuss how these norms affect the internal lives of at least one character.") Students were asked to post their responses on the Web site within their section discussion group each Thursday and, equally important, to read the posted responses of their section colleagues before they met in their smaller group discussion on Fridays. My pedagogical intent in this structure was twofold: to foster within each discussion section a sense of students participating in a writing community, and to increase student engagement and participation in discussions by having them think and write about the material before meeting with their peers to talk about it. Eight explanatory handouts with definitions, summaries, and questions to direct reading and thinking were posted for introductory lectures and for all novels and films to aid students in thinking and writing about the material each week. To assess students' responses to the material I met with the teaching assistants every third week to hear their reports on section discussions and to read student posts selected by the assistants to highlight issues and questions about instruction strategies that they wanted to discuss.

Content of the Course

As an English course, "Gender, Sexuality, Literature, and Culture" emphasizes the process and the power of reading texts (both novels and films) and learning to analyze the various strategies and structures of representation contained therein. Students are encouraged and given models about how to examine and analyze language itself (or visual language in the case of films) as a meaning-making system in which multiple and sometimes even divergent interpretations are elicited by and within a text. Adopting a queer theoretical methodology necessarily directs significant interrogation toward the concept and deployment of "normativity"—cultural norms and understandings that enforce certain social activities and identifications while actively preventing or punishing other activities that are perceived as falling outside said norms—as an organizing trope within texts. A queerly informed pedagogy then is a way into foregrounding attention to diverse permutations of norms within texts, what Britzman (1998) identifies as "methods of critiques to mark the repetitions of normalcy as a structure and as a pedagogy. Whether defining normalcy as an approximation of limits and mastery, or as renunciations, as the refusal of difference itself, Queer

Theory insists on posing the production of normalization as a problem of culture and of thought" (p. 214).

Although the novels—*The Shore of Women* (Sargent, 1986), *Graceland* (Abani, 2004), *In the Time of the Butterflies* (Alvarez, 1995), *Middlesex* (Eugenides, 2002)—and films—*Middle Sexes* (2006), *Ma Vie En Rose* (1997), *Foxfire* (1996), *Sex: Unknown* (2001)—in the course were chosen for their specific exploration of norms around both gender and sexuality, each text also presented a complex, intersecting web of social, historical, and political forces within which these norms acquired meaning and were both expressed and experienced in ways unique to the setting of each text.

Before students turned their attention to film and literary texts, I wanted to begin the course by introducing and simultaneously deconstructing the concept of norms, particularly with regard to sexuality and to gender. With this as the goal, I highlighted in the opening lecture my own misreading of the college-aged son of good friends, whom I had known since he was two. My own unconscious adherence to Western norms that equated gender expression with sexual orientation led me to assume that this boy was gay; his desire to dress for Halloween as a witch, his love of nail polish as a child, his insistence on taking a *My Little Pony* lunchbox to school, and his exclusive focus on a male friend during many of his pre-adolescent and teenage years constituted the evidence for my misreading. Though I informed the students that this young man began a relationship with a young woman during his senior year of high school that continued into his college years, I emphasized that even though my equation of his gender expression with sexual desire was proven incorrect, it would be equally erroneous to assume that we could declare him "heterosexual" forever because sexual expression can be fluid throughout a lifetime and because the hetero/homo binary does not, and cannot, encompass the range of sexual expression among human beings.

In the following lecture I began what I conceived of as an opening unit by introducing students to some of the contemporary theories informing gender and sexuality studies, including Foucault's (1978) analysis of how nineteenth century scientific discourses on sexuality created categories of "natural" and "unnatural" sexual practices, which simultaneously became criminalized and conflated with identities. This institutionalization of the "perverse" as a group rather than an attribute made a logical segue into Rich's (1980) coining of the term "compulsory heterosexuality," the idea that heterosexuality may not be innate, natural, or a preference, but is instead something that has had to be imposed, managed, organized, propagandized, and maintained by institutional coercion and pressure. From here we moved into Rubin's (1984) analysis of "sex panics" in American history, where certain marginalized groups are attacked and oppressed by the state, the medical profession, and by the media because they do not conform to current and dominant models of sexual acceptability or correctness. Rubin's argument is based upon what she terms the "sexual value system" in which she sees a hard line that separates "good" sex from both areas of contest and "bad" sex. In this formulation, "good sex" is considered to be normal, natural, healthy, and holy and it encompasses people who are heterosexual, married, reproductive, and have sex at home. "Areas of contest" are sexual situations and behaviors that are currently somewhere in between "good" sex and "bad" sex, and there is disagreement about whether or not the following should fit into the "good" or the "bad" category: unmarried heterosexual couples; promiscuous heterosexuals; masturbation; long-term, stable lesbian and gay male couples; lesbians in a bar; and promiscuous gay men at the baths or in a park. "Bad" sex is characterized by Rubin as something that society views as abnormal, unnatural, sick, sinful, and "way out," and encompasses the following groups and behaviors: transvestites, transsexuals and transgendered individuals, sado-masochists, people who have sex for money or prostitution, and cross-generational sex. Connected to Rubin's paradigm of the sexual value system is Sedgwick's (1984) list of sexual differences in which she argues that variations among people of identical gender, race, nationality, class, and sexual orientation have the potential to disrupt many of our available forms of thinking about sexuality. The examples of value-neutral differences she provides stand as counter-illustrations of the normativity-based "values" that Rubin (1984, pp. 25–26) critiques, and include such insights as:

- Even identical genital acts mean very different things to different people.
- To some people, what is sexual is bounded by genital acts; for others, it enfolds them or floats virtually free of them.
- Sexuality makes up a large share of the identity of some people, a small share of others' identity.
- Some people spend a lot of time thinking about sexuality, others little.
- Some people like to have a lot of sex; others little or none.

I ended this overview with Butler's (1990) concept of "gender performativity," what she argues are the daily, repeated attempts of any person to embody and conform to the gender norms in their culture. This repetitive performance of gender produces, according to Butler, the effect (what she would argue is an illusion) of a stable gender. Butler argues that there is no "true," "original," or "natural" gender identity behind the expressions (the performativity) of gender. Rather, in her scheme gender identity is "constituted by and through the very expressions that are claimed to be its results" (p. 25).

I followed this introduction of key concepts with a film showing of *Middle Sexes: Redefining He and She* (2006), a film that stresses the construction of what is "natural" within sexuality by examining both animal and human variations. The central theme within the film is uttered by Professor Milton H. Brown from the University of Hawaii: "One thing we have to remember from Darwin to Kinsey, to any great thinker about sexuality, is variation is the norm. Biology *loves* variation. Biology *loves* differences. Society *hates* it." The film also introduces global and cultural differences within sexual expression through a focus on *hijras*—identified as neither man nor woman in the culture of the Indian subcontinent—and *kathoeys*— a male-to-female transgendered person or an effeminate gay male in Thailand; *kathoeys* are also known as ladyboys and their sexual orientation is towards men, who themselves are not considered to be gay. Students were directed on the posted handout to pay particular attention to their emotional response to the film and to notice (without self-judgment) what parts or subjects made them uncomfortable. They were also asked to consider how the film defined and represented "nature," and to consider how this representation may have altered their conception of what is and can be seen as "natural."

Pamela Sargent's feminist novel *The Shore of Women* (1986) ended this first unit by encouraging students to examine cultural norms and how they shape and regulate constructs of gender and sexuality within a fictionalized dystopian future. What is both interesting and complex about this novel— and what makes it an efficacious teaching tool—is the inverted yet recognizable world it represents: women are in control of all advanced technology; they control their own reproduction as well as manipulate and contain men's sexuality; and they live in sex segregated homosocial and homosexual alliances that are perceived as utterly natural. They have adopted these conditions because of a past in which women suffered male predation through rape, physical violence, and a subordinate status that allowed them to be both bought and sold. A nuclear holocaust reverses the power relations and enforces a gendered essentialism on the part of the women who live protected in walled cities while the "bestial" men are consigned to roam outside in bands that are often engaged in violent survival struggles with one another for resources such as food and shelter. Sargent's novel follows the fate of one women exiled by her society who partners with a man for her survival and the way both must unlearn the norms they have believed to achieve a mutually respectful and equal relationship.

The Shore of Women provided students with an opportunity to explore sexuality, gender, religion, and cultural norms within an entirely fictional universe. The middle unit of the course—consisting of two novels and two films—shifted their critical focus to twentieth century texts and complex, contemporary permutations of these issues. Three of the texts were chosen because each recounted a coming-of-age tale in which the protagonist transitions from adolescence to adulthood in ways that are dictated according to a particular society and historical time. Chris Abani's novel *Graceland* (2004), for instance, charts not only shifts in time within the novel from the past (the rural village of Afikopo in the 1970s) to the present (Lagos in 1983), but it also explores Igbo rituals that confer manhood, women's status in Igbo and Nigerian society, cultural conceptions of what it is to be masculine, and the struggle of its protagonist, Elvis Oke, to balance his allegiance to, and comfort in, the world of women with that of his expected role as a young man. A character who both bridges and complicates binary gender roles—as a child he has a predilection for wearing make-up, he maintains relations with older women in his society about which male family members disapprove, and he works as a male escort in a club—Elvis also has a complicated and ambivalent relation to sexuality, including his attraction to an aunt, some subtle manifestations of same-sex desire, and a rape history by an adult male family member. Class and education also shape Elvis's choices throughout the novel, as much of his transition from youth to manhood necessarily involves economic survival in an urban setting (Lagos) and the life lessons he receives from a variety of male figures who represent a spectrum of choices about the ethics of survival in the rough and sometimes violent world of men.

Julia Alvarez's *In the Time of the Butterflies* (1995) also examines gender roles as they are shaped by historical (the Trujillo dictatorship and underground resistance), religious (Catholicism), and cultural (the expectation that all women will seek heterosexual marriages and motherhood) forces. Fictionalizing the intertwined stories of the four Mirabel sisters, Alvarez dramatizes life under authoritarian rule; the price one can pay for courage, resistance, and action; the flexibility of both gender roles and sexual desires when female heroism is demanded; and the power of the family in Dominican society. Family is also central to Alain Berliner's *Ma Vie En Rose* (1997) as a middle-class French family experiences the social ostracism and internal pressures that their transgendered son creates in their neatly ordered suburban life. The powerful mandate of social conventionality also figures in Annette Haywood-Carter's *Foxfire* (1996), where notions of female empowerment and solidarity in reaction to male violence are tested by gender nonconformity and the threat of same-sex attraction. In all of these texts, the attempt of protagonists to articulate individual expressions of sexuality and gender are inextricably intertwined with the historical pressures, as well as with the cultural and social norms within which they exist, thus necessitating an intersectional analytic frame for interpretation.

The final unit of the course focused on the liminal space between genders and sexualities through an examination of intersex individuals. The documentary *Sex Unknown* (2001) chronicles the life of Bruce Reimer, a male child whose penis is severed during a circumcision and whose parents are persuaded by the medical establishment to surgically alter him and raise him as a girl. Highlighting the power of the medical establishment to dictate what is considered normal genital formation and, by extension, gender assignment, the film explores the question of whether gender identity is cultural or biological and decides in favor of the latter. Jeffrey Eugenides' *Middlesex* (2002) explores these same issues through its intersex protagonist born with ambiguous genitalia, yet with a difference. Chronicling three generations of a Greek American immigrant family through major events (two World Wars and the Civil Rights, Women's Rights, and Gay Rights

Movements), the novel embeds its characters' transformations within the broader socio-historical changes that take place in the American twentieth century, representing its protagonist's struggle for selfhood and independence as a reflection of forces that both reference and construct her individual journey. In *Middlesex*, it is not just gender and sexuality that are thrown into crisis; all categories of identity—racial, class, ethnic, familial—are rendered as composite and nondiscrete. United States life, Eugenides seems to argue, is already liminal and unfettered by binaries, a melting pot where intersex is a metonymy for North American identity itself.

Outcomes

In anonymous student evaluations submitted at the end of the semester, course participants (209 reporting from an enrollment of 298) rated the course overall 4.21 (on a scale where 5 equals one of the best and 1 equals one of the worst). Positive evaluation of instructor preparation (4.83), clarity of course material (4.68), interest inspired in the subject matter (4.51), and high degrees of student participation (4.46) were also recorded. In individual comments, thirty-five students signaled their enjoyment of the books, seventeen of the films, and thirty students noted that they found the subject matter and class materials interesting. Thirty students felt that there was too much reading assigned during the semester.

Several students (eleven) also commented on how this course had introduced them to information about which they had been unaware, how "delicate" and "touchy" many of the issues raised in the course were (eight), and one student went so far as to declare that "This should be a mandatory Gen-Ed for all incoming freshmen." Students (eight) also expressed their appreciation for the multiple perspectives and cultural diversity in the course, and one wrote that "I want to visit the Dominican Republic now, and I think that's impressive inspiration for an English Gen Ed." Only one evaluation voiced negative comments about the course material, expressed as "the vulgarity of the videos" and "Don't like the gay material."

As the evaluations indicate, college-age students (no doubt because of their own life-stage issues around independence and sexual identity) were intrigued by the course material and open to explorations of gender and sexuality as they were expressed in different cultural, national, familial, religious, class, and historical formulations. A queerly informed pedagogy offers the tools to deconstruct norms and to situate differences within multiple vectors of identity not restricted exclusively to gender and sexuality.

References

Abani, C. *Graceland*. New York: Picador, 2004.
Alvarez, J. *In the Time of the Butterflies*. New York: Plume, 1995.

Berlant, L., and others (eds.), *Forum: On the Political Implications of Using the Term 'Queer,' as in 'Queer Politics,' 'Queer Studies,' and 'Queer Pedagogy.' Radical Teacher,* 1994, *45,* 52–57.

Britzman, D. P. "Is There a Queer Pedagogy? Or Stop Reading Straight." In W. F. Pinar (ed.), *Curriculum: Toward New Identities.* New York: Garland Publishing, 1998.

Butler, J. *Gender Trouble.* New York: Routledge, 1990.

Eugenides, J. *Middlesex.* New York: Picador, 2002.

Foucault, M. *The History of Sexuality.* Vol. 1, *An Introduction.* Translated by R. Hurley. New York: Vintage, 1978.

Foxfire. Directed by A. Haywood-Carter. Santa Monica, Calif.: Rysher Entertainment, 1996, Video DVD.

Hall, D. "Introduction: Queer Works." *College English,* 1997, *24*(1), 2–10.

Holmes, M. M. "Chalkdusting." In L. Berlant, and others (eds.), *Forum: On the Political Implications of Using the Term 'Queer,' as in 'Queer Politics,' 'Queer Studies,' and 'Queer Pedagogy.' Radical Teacher,* 1994, *45,* 52–57.

Jagose, A. *Queer Theory: An Introduction.* New York: New York University Press, 1996.

Kirsch, M. K. *Queer Theory and Social Change.* New York: Routledge, 2000.

Lovass, K. E., Elia, J. P., and Yep, G. A. "Introduction." In *LGBT Studies and Queer Theory: New Conflicts, Collaborations, and Contested Terrain.* New York: Harrington Park Press, 2006.

Ma Vie En Rose. Directed by A. Berliner. Culver City, CA: Sony Pictures, 1997, Video DVD.

Middle Sexes: Redefining He and She. Directed by A. Thomas. New York: Home Box Office, 2006, Video DVD.

Rich, A. (1980). "Compulsory Heterosexuality and Lesbian Existence." In H. Abelove, M. A. Barale, and D. M. Halperin (eds.), *The Lesbian and Gay Studies Reader.* New York: Routledge, 1993.

Rubin, G. "Thinking Sex: Notes for a Radical Theory of the Politics of Sexuality." In C. Vance (ed.), *Pleasure and Danger.* Boston: Routledge and Kegan Paul, 1984.

Sargent, P. *The Shore of Women.* Dallas: Benbella Books, 1986.

Sedgwick, E. *Epistemology of the Closet.* Berkeley: University of California Press, 1984.

Sedgwick, E. *Tendencies.* Durham, N.C.: Duke University Press, 1993.

Seidman, S. "Deconstructing Queer Theory or the Under-Theorization of the Social and the Ethical." In L. Nicholson and S. Seidman (eds.), *Social Postmodernism: Beyond Identity Politics.* Cambridge, U.K.: Cambridge University Press, 1995.

Sex: Unknown. Directed by A. Ritsko. London: British Broadcasting Corporation, 2001, VHS Videotape.

Slagle, R. A. "Ferment in LGBT Studies and Queer Theory: Personal Ruminations on Contested Terrain." In K. E. Lovass, J. P. Elia, and G. A. Yep (eds.), *LGBT Studies and Queer Theory: New Conflicts, Collaborations, and Contested Terrain.* New York: Harrington Park Press, 2006.

DEBORAH CARLIN is a professor of American literary and cultural studies at the University of Massachusetts Amherst.

NEW DIRECTIONS FOR TEACHING AND LEARNING • DOI: 10.1002/tl

The author advocates teaching trans issues from an intersectional systems-based perspective. This framework helps students to understand that "trans issues" are about more than individual identity, body modification, and a need for tolerance. This perspective can also help to move "trans issues" out of its current position as a "special topic" within the margins of a few select disciplines.

Teaching "Trans Issues": An Intersectional and Systems-Based Approach

Michel J. Boucher

Transgender people are becoming increasingly visible in popular culture, academia, and national politics. They have appeared on *The Oprah Winfrey Show* and *The Real World*; on a variety of cable network programs such as *Discovery*, *A & E*, and *The L Word*; and in televised interviews with Barbara Walters and Dr. Oz. National Public Radio (NPR) has produced numerous stories on trans issues, and there have been a variety of articles on trans people in *The New York Times* and other major newspapers and magazines. Memoirs written by trans people are often available in mainstream bookstore giants such as Barnes and Noble and Borders, and sometimes gain national attention. For example, Jennifer Finney Boylan's *She's Not There* (2003) and Deidre McCloskey's *Crossing* (1999) are memoirs written by university faculty members who are transsexual women. By sharing their stories, they have brought trans issues into open discussion among their institutional and disciplinary colleagues.

University and college administrators are struggling at every level with how to address the needs of trans-identified staff people, faculty members, and students, all of whom are increasingly becoming open, vibrant participants in university communities. Across the nation, trans students also are pushing university administrators to address the ways in which institutions of higher education, like most institutions in the United States, systematically marginalize and often exclude trans people from full participation in college and university life (Beemyn, Curtis, Davis, and Tubbs, 2005). At the University of Massachusetts Amherst, where I work and earned my doctorate, the administration has faced pressure both from students and from the Stonewall Center (the university's gay, lesbian, bisexual, and transgender center) to include gender identity and expression in their non-discrimination clause, to turn single-sex bathrooms on campus into unisex ones, to accommodate the gender of trans students in housing assignments, and to create bathroom and locker room spaces that can be safely used by trans students in newly constructed buildings, including the new student recreation facility. Despite such progress, university administrators often resist these changes and view "trans issues" as identity "problems" of a very small number of students (Gershenson, 2009). This is partially an effect of the ways in which "trans issues" have been framed in popular culture and academia as identity issues rather than as systemic and institutional productions and problems.

Trans activists, scholars, and their allies have also have raised important questions about the ways "trans issues" are framed in a number of disciplines (Burdge, 2007; Reiss, 2004). Historically understood as a psychological pathology, and still frequently framed in this way, "trans issues," until recently, have been predominantly situated within psychology classes as a "disorder" or sexual "deviance" when addressed at all. As transgender identity increasingly becomes understood as a social identity of an oppressed minority, the framing of trans identity in academia is changing and professors from across disciplines are thinking about how to incorporate "trans issues" in non-pathological ways within their own course curriculums. Like the Women's Studies department at the University of Massachusetts Amherst, which last year became Women, Gender, Sexuality Studies, Women's Studies departments throughout the country are changing their names to reflect an analytical shift within the discipline from "women" to "gender."

Given these conditions, it is useful to think critically about the conceptual frameworks that are used to represent, define, and address "trans issues" and the effects of these framings for trans people. Most undergraduate students will have gleaned their understanding of transgender issues and identities from popular culture representations, most likely television talk shows, television sitcoms, reality shows, or popular films. As a result, students will be tempted to consistently channel classroom discussion toward questions about the bodies of trans people, the effects of surgeries or hormones, debates about whether or not transsexual people are obligated to tell others about their transsexuality if they otherwise "pass," and whether one can ever really change one's gender. Instructors must consciously offer students a different framework for thinking about transgender issues, or classroom discussions will likely mirror the content and form of these larger cultural debates.

In this chapter, I argue that an intersectional systems-based framework for teaching "trans issues" can help students understand that this topic extends beyond individual identities, forms and effects of physical transition, and prejudices that can be fixed by an increase in tolerance. Students come to see how institutional policies and practices undergird and reinforce social prejudices in ways that have severe social and economic repercussions for most gender non-conforming people and exacerbate race and class inequalities. This approach can also facilitate a shift in the position of "trans issues" as marginal, special issues topics in a few disciplines to an incorporation of "trans issues" as part of a variety of courses taught across the disciplines.

Teacher as Text

I have been teaching at the University of Massachusetts Amherst for over ten years as a teaching associate, lecturer, and adjunct professor. I began my teaching career at UMass Amherst as a graduate student and as a white woman. During my time as a graduate student, I came out as transgender and transitioned to living and identifying as a trans man. I have been an active participant at UMass Amherst in working to improve conditions for trans students. As a teacher in both the English department and the Women, Gender, Sexuality Studies Program, I have students that take my courses to fulfill a departmental requirement or because the topic speaks to their own lives or identities.

Though I have taught a range of courses and in a variety of contexts, for this chapter I draw mostly from my experiences in designing and teaching courses on gender, sexuality, and queer studies. I also pull from my experiences as a trans activist, graduate employee of the Stonewall Center, guest lecturer on "trans issues" in classes within and outside of the local five colleges, and as an experienced facilitator of numerous workshops for university administrators, health care professionals, and employment agencies on "trans issues." Depending upon the class and the course content, or workshop context, I sometimes choose to "come out" as trans and at other times I do not. Students are often surprised to find out that I am a trans man, but rarely have I met any direct, negative reactions. Although one does not need to be trans to teach these issues, a department that supports the visibility of trans professors and students is a significant step toward incorporating trans issues into course curriculums in ways that resist, and even combat, the pathologization of trans identities.

Defining Terms

Defining "trans," "transgender," and "transsexual" is a complicated task. It is easy for classroom discussions to get stuck on defining and understanding the variety of identities that fall under the umbrella term 'transgender.' I usually begin by saying that I will define these terms in a general way, but that I then want to move on to discussing the institutional and systemic issues faced by trans people. The first point I make during this part of the discussion is that dominant discourse naturalizes what can be understood as culturally produced linear links between sex (the biological features used to define one as male, female, or intersex at birth), gender (social expectations and roles of male and female people, and one's internal understanding of oneself as a man, woman, or some other category), and sexuality (straight, gay, bisexual). It is presumed that, except for rare occurrences, all people can easily be categorized as male or female at birth, and that there is a "natural" progression between sex and gender identity such that a male automatically grows up to identify as a man (preferably masculine) and a female automatically grows up to identify as a woman (preferably feminine). I suggest to students that they bracket such beliefs at least temporarily to entertain the idea that this configuration of sex/gender might not be the only "natural" one. Trans and gender non-conforming activists call into question the "natural" links between biological birth sex and gender identity (Feinberg, 1999). Trans or gender non-conforming people are those whose gender expressions do not fit within this naturalized trajectory, particularly the presumed link between biological sex and gender identity or expression.

I use the phrases trans and gender non-conforming people because, as David Valentine (2007) points out, "transgender" and/or "transsexual" are not terms that all gender non-conforming people use to describe themselves, even when they might be categorized as trans by medical professionals or social service agencies. Identity categories are used differently by different individuals, and conceptual configurations of the relationships between sex, gender, and sexuality often shift across race and class lines. The main goal for me is not to explain and define every transgender identity, but to emphasize that all of the identity terms trans and gender non-conforming people use to describe themselves are contextual and in flux.

With the term 'intersectional perspective,' I am referring to a theoretical framework developed primarily by women of color feminists (Combahee River Collective, 1995) to account for the ways in which race, gender, class, and sexuality are discourses and identities that are always being shaped by and formed through each other. In a feminist context, intersectional perspectives centralize difference rather than commonality between women as a core framework for analysis. An intersectional analysis of power is one that understands the operations of power as multi-layered, with each "layer" always both shaping and in fact depending upon the other.

Teaching Trans Issues from an Intersectional and a Systems Framework

To help students think about trans issues as institutional issues rather than simply as individual identity-based ones, I begin with personal reflective writing and low-risk discussion topics. This allows me to assess their readiness and current knowledge, to learn more about them as individuals, and to help students prepare for the more challenging material to come. I often ask students to write in response to a two-part question: (1) What is your gender and how do you know? How did you learn that you are the gender you claim? (2) If your gender was on trial, how would you prove your gender is what you say it is? What kind of evidence can you offer? These questions can take the form of a quick, in-class free write or a longer assignment where the instructor asks them to use these questions as a guide for writing a longer gender history of their lives, which might be particularly appropriate for students training to be social workers or psychologists. Ultimately, they serve two purposes: First, unlike non-trans people who rarely find themselves being asked to explain how they know their gender and how they came to be a particular gender, trans people often find themselves in the position of having to "prove" that they really are the gender to which they lay claim with very few stable, non-stereotypical resources to draw from to substantiate their claims. These questions force non-trans students into the position of having to justify and prove their gender, and can highlight the ways in which normative gender has become unquestionably "natural."

After students begin to see that normative gender carries the unquestioned experience of "naturalness" and "realness," I can begin to highlight some of the ways that this "naturalness" is produced, enforced, and maintained through institutional architecture, legal documents, and everyday social and institutional practices. In a way that both manifests and secures dominant gender ideology as "natural," one's legal identity as a man or woman is established by the characteristics of one's body at birth and this designation is written on all of one's documents. It determines who one can marry, the type of prison one is assigned to if convicted of a crime, and the locker rooms and bathrooms one can legally use. It is reported to places of employment by the Social Security department, it is on medical and education records, and it is used as a signifier of identity on passports and driver's licenses. Because the concept that one's "real" gender is determined by one's biological sex is so deeply entrenched as the only "natural" configuration of gender, those whose sex and gender coincide with cultural standards are automatically conferred with gendered "realness." In contrast, and interdependently, those who "cross" genders are seen to be performing a gender that is not "real" (Bettcher, 2007).

When students are able to see that dominant ideologies of gendered "realness" are not necessarily "natural" and that it might just as legitimately take other forms, I can move forward with a feminist analysis of trans issues that begins with the assumption that trans identities are as "real" and legitimate as non-trans identities. This sets the stage for the next teaching module, which highlights a cycle of institutional exclusion of trans people, which is perpetuated through racial and class inequalities and re-creates these distinctions within trans communities.

Institutional Exclusion of Trans People. Although the questions I first introduce focus on individual identity, they work as a pathway into an analysis of trans issues as institutionally structured. When students are asked in classroom discussion how they know or learned their gender, someone almost always very quickly cites their genitals as proof of their gender, to which I usually respond, how did you come to understand that genitals determine whether one is a boy or a girl? Many students remember specific stories about learning that their genitals define them as girls or boys, usually taught by family or peers, and learning about particular gender characteristics that were supposed to go along with their gender assignment. Commonly students say, "the doctor decided," or "my parents told me," or "I learned in school" or the "media." Soon, I have a list on the board of institutions that teach, reproduce, and naturalize the idea that one's "real" gender is that which is assigned to them at birth according to their genitals.

Next, to highlight the institutional regulation of gender normativity, I ask students what would happen or what they have witnessed happening to a person whose gender expression is outside of dominant norms or if a person claims to be a gender other than that which they were assigned at birth. Most students can recall a time when they or a peer in school was teased, harassed, or assaulted due to their gender expression. Schools are institutions with which students are intimately familiar, so a discussion of school experiences sets a foundation from which a macro-level analysis of trans issues can be built. It creates a context for students to think about institutions as places that regulate gender through their structure and the actions that take place and are implicitly, if not explicitly, sanctioned there. The architectural settings of schools passively affirm normative gender role expectations and behaviors while providing a context wherein the bodies of those who do not conform are highlighted. For example, bathrooms and locker rooms subject students to heightened scrutiny and are often places where gender non-conforming students are attacked (Gershenson, 2009; Meteik and Sylvia Rivera Law Project, 2003).

To help facilitate the move from personal anecdotes to institutional analysis, I assign readings that link what students may have witnessed or experienced in their own lives to research data that describes the aggregate experiences of many trans people in schools and which highlight the exclusion of and violence against trans people within schools as a widespread problem with serious long-term economic and psychological effects. For example, Wyss (2005) has found that 86 percent of the high school students in her study experienced physical assaults at school. Her research subjects describe a range of assaults such as being pushed down stairs, set on fire, and raped in school bathrooms. Given these conditions in secondary school settings, it is not surprising that a significant percentage of trans people drop out of high school before completing their degree (Xavier, Bobbin, Singer, and Budd, 2005). Trans students are, through harassment and physical assaults, literally expelled from the student body and the institutional space of the school.

Most students understand the direct connection between education and employment that provides a living wage. Having first understood the ways that trans students are literally expelled from schools through harassment and violence, students will be able to connect this to economic and class implications such as the high unemployment rate and job discrimination that trans people face. Recent studies across race and class lines show an unemployment rate among trans people that ranges from thirty-five to fifty percent unemployed (Clements-Nolle, Marx, and Katz, 2001). In one report as many as 59 percent of transgender workers reported experiencing job discrimination and 49 percent had never been offered a job living as a transgender person (Make the Road New York, 2010).

The research data I present to students helps illuminate that the daily process of harassment and violence aimed at trans people and their exclusion from the social body is not made up of random, individual acts of violence or prejudice. Rather, dominant gender ideology is produced and enforced through institutional structures and the institutionally supported policing of public space, sometimes passively and sometimes quite actively. Like schools, other public settings such as hospitals, public restrooms, public gym facilities, homeless and domestic violence shelters, dormitories, clothing stores, prisons, and places of employment are all architecturally and structurally designed in ways that produce and affirm gendered normativity while highlighting non-normative genders as "not real," as not belonging. Often, students comment that they have never thought about the structures of institutions in this way. Research shows that the exclusion and violence experienced by students in schools extends into public space where gender normativity is monitored and enforced through violence and harassment aimed at trans people (Stotzer, 2009). As one student explained to Wyss (2005), " 'I just walked around the world really, really afraid [. . .], jus' feelin' like, 'Someone's gonna' kill me' " (p. 719).

My next task is to help students understand how race and class dynamics have a major role in determining the extent of social and economic marginalization that trans people face. Although there is little legal protection for any trans person against discrimination in housing, employment, or any other form, race and class privilege can help to mediate some of the most severe repercussions of living as a gender non-normative person. Those who come out as trans later in life and who come from economic backgrounds that have enabled them to gain professional employment have often had an opportunity to establish support systems and economic stability before they come out as trans, both of which help mediate the social and economic repercussions of living as a gender non-conforming person. In contrast, racism and class disadvantage make it extremely difficult for trans people of color or without class advantage to find employment, often forcing low-income trans people, especially

NEW DIRECTIONS FOR TEACHING AND LEARNING • DOI: 10.1002/tl

low-income trans people of color, to "drop out of the formal economy entirely" (Make the Road New York, 2010, p. 9; Park, 2003). Job discrimination is exacerbated by one's visibility as a trans person, which can be mediated with hormones and surgeries that are often legally accessible only to those who have class advantage. This fact leads us into the next module where we explore how socio-economic pressures can lead many trans people into conflict with other social institutions such as the legal system, which then intensifies and reinforces the social and economic marginalization they experience.

Race, Class, and the Snowball Effect of Exclusion

One of my main teaching goals when addressing "trans issues" is to help students understand the perpetual cycle of institutional exclusion that leads to severe social and economic marginalization for trans people whose class and race status cannot mediate these effects. Through this module, students will come to understand that when trans people are excluded from employment opportunities through lack of education and racial, class, and gender discrimination, they become even more vulnerable to social and institutional violence, this time at the hands of police officers and within the prison system.

Mirroring general trends of police brutality against communities of color in the US, the findings of an Amnesty International Report (2005) "strongly indicate that transgender people, people from ethnic and racial minorities, young people, sex workers and immigrants within the LGBT community experience heightened risk for abuse by law enforcement officials" (p. 39). In a study of ethnic minority trans youth ages sixteen to twenty-five (Garofalo and others, 2006), 59 percent of participants reported engaging in sex in exchange for resources, 63 percent reported having trouble finding a job, and only a little over a half were either employed or in school. Out of those who reported a history of sex work, 90 percent also had a history of incarceration.

For students to grasp the systemic manifestation of trans oppression, it is important to highlight that police harassment, arrests, and the incarceration of trans people, particularly of low income and/or trans women of color, is sustained through both institutional exclusion and the illegal status of sex work, one of the few areas of employment that remains consistently open to trans people (Namaste, 2005). Once in prison, trans people are commonly victims of orchestrated sexual assaults and other forms of violence, making police harassment and abuse of trans people in prison two of the most urgent issues that trans people face (Sylvia Rivera Law Project 2007; Amnesty International, 2005).

It is in this teaching module that I find it most useful to use personal narratives to highlight the violence and exclusion many trans people face on a daily basis. Excellent individual narratives can be found in the Sylvia

Rivera Law Project report, "It's War in Here" and in "Stonewalled" by Amnesty International. I only rarely share personal narratives. Although trans people are often expected to discuss trans issues in relation to their personal lives and bodies, when they do, they are also often criticized for "seeking attention" or sharing "too much information." Trans instructors, in particular, can be accused of having personal agendas in teaching trans issues, so I find that it helps to minimize this criticism when I present students with the narratives of other trans people, particularly those that are recorded in well-documented research reports that illuminate societal patterns of violence and oppression. These are the narratives that are absent in the news reports, memoirs, popular and documentary film, and television programs with which students tend to be most familiar. So, if I use individual narratives to teach "trans issues" at all, I do it in a way that highlights institutional oppression rather than the autobiographical narratives of trans people and their physical transitions.

Integrating Trans Issues

Helping students to break away from imagining trans issues as identity issues that are separate from other topics in the social sciences and humanities is a major challenge. In my Women's Studies classes, I continue to introduce trans issues when covering topics such as marriage, reproductive justice, sexual violence, migration, and globalization to model an integrated approach to teaching trans issues. As I conference with students about their own research topics, I encourage them to apply a framework of analysis that reflects the integral relationship between trans and feminist issues. For instance, if a student is interested in learning about domestic violence, I ask them to consider how the ideology of gendered "realness" and fear of police intervention might help to create conditions within which domestic violence against trans people can thrive. Are domestic violence hotlines and shelters structured so as to accommodate trans victims of domestic violence, and if not, how does this institutional exclusion help support domestic violence in trans communities. How might these organizations expand or reorganize their philosophy and their services to include trans people? The same types of questions and inquiries can be applied to almost any topic that is traditionally taught within the social sciences and humanities. This framework helps students to see that within their own fields of interest and potential employment contexts, they can help to shift the discursive and institutional environments that produce the violence and social and economic exclusion that are at the heart of trans issues.

Conclusion

If our cultural understanding of "trans issues" is going to move beyond a voyeuristic examination of trans identities and bodies, educators must shift our conceptual paradigms and teaching strategies. An intersectional model and systems-based analysis provides a way for students to move away from debating the "realness" of trans identities and bodies to analyzing and understanding how institutions monitor and regulate gender through already well-worn tracks of race and class inequalities and in doing so exacerbate these entrenched disparities. Higher education has an important opportunity and responsibility to help lead cultural and institutional change. When students enter the workforce with an understanding of "trans issues" as institutional problems, they are more likely to help create the structural transformations that are necessary for trans and gender nonconforming people to be able to participate more fully in our economic and social systems. Institutional structures and educational environments that recognize trans students and educators as valid and vital participants in our educational systems will model this change process for students. An intersectional and systems-based emphasis also helps students to think critically about how normative ideologies and social inequalities related to gender, race, and sexuality are institutionally produced and not necessarily "natural" configurations of social life or effects of individual characteristics. This perspective gives them new information about gender and its intersections with race, class, and sexuality and, perhaps more importantly, provides them with new ways to think about our social arrangements and imagine different possibilities. These imaginative and critical thinking skills will be keys to their ability to participate in ongoing social transformation and the enactment of social justice.

References

Amnesty International. "Stonewalled: Police Abuse and Misconduct against Lesbian, Gay and Transgender People in the US." New York: Amnesty International, 2005.

Beemyn, B., Curtis, B., Davis, M., and Tubbs, N. J. "Transgender Issues on College Campuses." In Gender Identity and Sexual Orientation: Research, Policy, and Personal Perspectives. New Directions for Student Services, no. 111. San Francisco: Jossey-Bass, 2005, 49–60.

Bettcher, T. M. "Evil Deceivers and Make-Believers: On Transphobic Violence and the Politics of Illusion." Hypatia, 2007, 22, 44–65.

Boylan, J. F. She's Not There: A Life in Two Genders. New York: Broadway, 2003.

Burdge, B. "Bending Gender, Ending Gender: Theoretical Foundations for Social Work Practice with the Transgender Community." Social Work, 2007, 51(3), 243–250.

Clements-Nolle, K., Marx, R., and Katz, M. "HIV Prevalence, Risk Behaviors, Health Care and Mental Health Status of Transgendered Persons: Implications for Public Health Intervention." American Journal of Public Health, 2001, 91(6), 915–921.

Combahee River Collective. "A Black Feminist Statement." In B. Guy-Sheftall (ed.), Words of Fire: An Anthology of African-American Feminist Thought. New York: The New Press, 1995.

Feinberg, L. Transliberation: Beyond Pink and Blue. Boston: Beacon, 1999.

Garofalo, and others. "Overlooked, Misunderstood and At-Risk: Exploring the Lives and HIV Risk of Ethnic Minority Male-to-Female Transgender Youth." Journal of Adolescent Health, 2006, 38, 230–236.

Gershenson, O. "Introduction." In O. Gershenson (ed.), *Ladies and Gents: Public Toilets and Gender*. Philadelphia: Temple University Press, 2009.

Make the Road New York. "Transgender Need Not Apply: A Report on Transgender Job Discrimination." New York: Make the Road NY, 2010. Retrieved August 30, 2010, from http://www.maketheroad.org

McCloskey, D. N. *Crossing: A Memoir*. Chicago: University of Chicago Press, 1999.

Meteik, T., and Sylvia Rivera Law Project. *Toilet Training*. New York: Sylvia Rivera Law Project, 2003, Video DVD.

Namaste, V. *Sex Change, Social Change: Reflections on Identity, Institutions, and Imperialism*. Toronto: Women's Press, 2005.

Park, Ji Hoon (director). *I Am Who I Am*. 2003, Video DVD, (aired on WYBE PBS in PA on February 18, 2004).

Reiss, E. "Teaching Transgender History, Identity, and Politics." *Radical History Review*, 2004, *88*, 166–177.

Stotzer, R. "Violence Against Transgender People: A Review of United States Data." *Aggression and Violent Behavior*, 2009, *14*(3), 170–179.

Sylvia Rivera Law Project. " 'It's War in Here': A Report on the Treatment of Transgender and Intersex People in New York State Men's Prisons." New York: Sylvia Rivera Law Project, 2007. Retrieved August 30, 2010, from http://srlp.org/files/warinhere.pdf

Valentine, D. *Imagining Transgender: An Ethnography of a Category*. Durham, N.C.: Duke University Press, 2007.

Wyss, S. E. " 'This Was My Hell': The Violence Experienced by Gender Non-Conforming Youth in US High Schools." *International Journal of Qualitative Studies in Education*, 2005, *17*(5), 709–730.

Xavier, J., Bobbin, M., Singer, B., and Budd, E. "A Needs Assessment of Transgendered People of Color Living in Washington, DC." *International Journal of Transgenderism*, 2005, *8*(2/3), 31–47.

MICHEL J. BOUCHER is an adjunct professor in the Women, Gender, Sexuality Studies Department and the English Department at the University of Massachusetts Amherst.

7

The authors present specific challenges, possibilities, and critical intersections that have emerged in their teaching and learning with both refugees and veterans in Asian American studies courses.

Refugees, Veterans, and Continuing Pedagogies of PTSD in Asian American Studies

Shirley Suet-ling Tang, Peter Nien-chu Kiang

In this chapter, we describe how a pedagogical commitment at one urban public school to support teaching and learning with Southeast Asian refugee students and their Vietnam veteran classmates two decades ago has continued to be meaningful for more recently arrived refugee students from other world regions as well as for a diverse, new generation of student veterans who are facing their own issues of trauma and post-traumatic stress disorder (PTSD). In sharing aspects of our own pedagogical practice—our pedagogies of PTSD—we present some of the challenges, possibilities, and critical intersections that have emerged in our work with both refugees and veterans in the classroom.

Refugee Realities and Reflections

In previous work, Kiang has written extensively about the intersecting, multidimensional identities as well as the distinct strengths, needs, and survival strategies that characterize the persistence of Southeast Asian American students as refugees, as immigrants, and as racial minorities in school (Kiang, 1995, 1996). Kiang's work has also highlighted the transformative role of Asian American studies courses to "educate for life" through both curriculum content and "pedagogies of life and death" that have provided circles of healing, not only for refugees, but also for student veterans,

NEW DIRECTIONS FOR TEACHING AND LEARNING, no. 125, Spring 2011 © Wiley Periodicals, Inc.
Published online in Wiley Online Library (wileyonlinelibrary.com) • DOI: 10.1002/tl.435

particularly Vietnam veterans, in the classroom (Kiang, 1997, 2002, 2003a).

From the 1980s to the present, our campus has enrolled the highest percentage of both Vietnamese students and US veterans of any university in New England. Veterans and refugees often sit side-by-side in Asian American studies courses such as the Southeast Asians in the US course, which we have offered at least once each year since 1989. Although grounding this course in multidisciplinary content focusing on legacies of the Vietnam War, we have, from the beginning, also conceptualized and intentionally structured our learning environments to address trauma and support healing in relation to our students' lives.

To illustrate how students experience this kind of learning environment, we offer the following two excerpts from end-of-semester written reflections by Vietnamese refugee students. The first reveals a female student's painful, but purposeful engagement with the course content:

> I cried most when the professor showed a video of a small boat with some fifty people escaped from Vietnam and reading from "Lone Pink Fish" about Vietnamese at sea. Pains rose within me when I saw the faces of those people and the images that were described in the reading. I am crying now as I write . . . I wasn't ready or prepared for such scenes. I tried so hard to bury the pain and hopelessness of the escape for years. I thought that my wounds had heal but when I watch the video and do the reading, I felt like someone had took a knife and slash the healing wound open again. I felt that my tears were no different from the blood that was running down from my wounds. Although upset, I was glad that the professor showed the video and have such reading. If it wasn't for that, our struggles and hardships would forever remain silence and no one would ever understand what we had to go through (Kiang, 2003b, p. 206).

In the second excerpt, a male student from a different semester explains the therapeutic importance of peer interactions through the classroom environment:

> The student who gave a presentation about the Cambodian temple approached me and held out his right hand to shake my hand. He said to me, "You know, I really appreciate your immigrant story . . . I appreciate your courage to tell us about it, and I am really sorry that it happened to you." But he said this very slowly, and I looked into his eyes and tears were coming out . . . I have never touched anyone in my life, but this time I really did . . . we shared some jokes and work stories, and three hours later I found myself in my room. Everything became silent and all of sudden I started to cry . . . I couldn't sleep the whole night. I woke up at 2:00am with all thoughts overflowing in my mind and decided to write this memo. The videos, the field trip, the "boat people SOS" [video] brought back all the

memories. It was the most meaningful experience for me. I miss the laughter, the beautiful faces, and the migration stories . . . I will use this class as guide to help me help others who are in need (Kiang, 2003b, pp. 206–207).

These rich examples of course-based reflective writing—just two among thousands we have collected—suggest specific elements that we view as essential in our pedagogies of PTSD:

- Connecting formal (and powerful) course content with personal experiences, particularly in analyzing loss, recognizing struggle, and valuing life
- Providing consistent time/space through assigned activities for individual reflection and collective sharing of personal narratives
- Enabling and modeling caring interactions with diverse peers
- Internalizing long-term commitments to make positive changes that help others

New Generations and Continuing Legacies

Given dramatic generational turnings in our student body during the past decade from those who directly experienced war in Southeast Asia as refugees and veterans to their college-aged children, we have purposefully structured family/community research assignments that enable current students to gather stories about migration histories or name origins from older family members and community elders, as illustrated in this example:

> The name "Rath" or "Ratha" was given by my father. It was unfortunate for me that I never have a chance to know why my father chose this name for me because my father was killed when I was at the age of three. However, I did find out some details from my mother about my name. She told me that the reason was picked partly because I was born during the war. Everyone was running for refuge at the time of the war. In Khmer language the word running is pronounced somewhat similar to my name (Kiang, 2003a, p. 210).

By encouraging both the gathering and sharing of what we refer to as "real life real stories" (Tang and Bui, 2009; Tang, 2008b), these migration story and name story assignments infuse educational purpose and publicly recognized academic value to domains of experience that are more typically private and personal among students and families—often with healing effects (Lin, Suyemoto, and Kiang, 2009). The individual research process, compilation of emerging products, and cumulative sharing of reflective learning represent consistent practices in our pedagogy. In addition, we continually design fresh interventions—using oral history, service-learning, kindergarten through twelfth grade engagement, community documentation, media literacy, and multimedia production—to address the realities of our U.S.-born

Southeast Asian American students and their classmates who often face their own traumatic losses resulting from urban violence both within a group and across different groups of youth of color, as shown in the next section.

Intersections with Urban Violence

At the beginning of a new school year in 2003, we found ourselves in the midst of planning for a vigil and healing ceremony that would bring together different generations of local residents from Boston's North Shore region, including teachers, community organizers, activist artists, and a multi-ethnic group of Khmer (Cambodian), Latino, black and white youth. Organized primarily by young adults in the community, including many of our school's Khmer American students at that time, the healing ceremony represented our collective response to the shooting of a Khmer American young man at a nearby public beach. A four-sentence newspaper brief had reported the killing and described the motive as gang member rivalries (Alleged Gang Fight Results in Death, 2003). But the victim was not a gang member, and those who knew him wanted his story clarified and his memory respected (Medaglia, 2003).

At the ceremony along the beach, we shared in traditional rituals led by monks from the neighborhood's Khmer Buddhist temple. Friends then recalled how the young man had fostered friendships with people from different backgrounds in a neighborhood struggling with legacies of war as well as barriers of racism, poverty, and language. Elders referenced connections between inter-ethnic violence, school failure, and racial harassment from earlier years of refugee resettlement. Teens marched with hand-painted banners to express their rage at so much injustice in their world.

Prior to his death, the Khmer American young man had struggled economically and educationally, like many first-generation students at our urban public school. Having just completed his general equivalency diploma, he had intended to visit our campus the following week to see what Asian American studies courses he might take in the future. His tragic death brought confusion and guilt to many of the community's young people, including our students who began to question the purpose of their own educational plans. At the ceremony, though, they found some answers by standing together in a circle of remembrance, honor, and healing. In this pedagogical example, the relevant learning environment shifted from the classroom to the community where we offered respect and collectively transformed the actual site of the killing.

For the remainder of that semester, students in the Southeast Asians in the US course worked intensively to complete a range of group research projects that directly responded to this traumatic loss by analyzing the educational needs of Khmer American students in the neighborhood, documenting voices and experiences of street-involved youth in the region, and critiquing dominant perceptions and policies that unfairly framed

NEW DIRECTIONS FOR TEACHING AND LEARNING • DOI: 10.1002/tl

community violence in local Southeast Asian American communities (Tang, 2008a). The depth, scope, and quality of students' projects clearly reflected their internalization of the urgent need for their work.

Intersections with New Generation Refugees

The Southeast Asians in the US course developed originally by Kiang in 1989 and taught primarily by Tang since 2000 continues to be a space that allows recent refugee students to process and share their own experiences with war, trauma, and healing, albeit from countries such as Guatemala, Haiti, Liberia, Iran, and elsewhere. For example, after viewing an excerpt from *Hearts and Minds*, the 1974 film documentary by Peter Davis about the Vietnam War, a Lebanese student wrote in a freewrite reflection, "my memory takes me back to my country. The same views still stuck in my eyes . . . especially those burnt kids in one of the video reminded me about my best friend who died last year, not too long ago. I still can see him right in front of me like it's now when they brought him after the accident. He died in one of the bombs while going to his work."

In another semester, at the end of the first two weeks of lectures and video presentations about the war in Southeast Asia, a married Sudanese couple who had fled their country's civil war for a refugee camp in Kenya before moving to the United States broke the silence to initiate class discussion. First, with a big smile and steady gaze, the husband noted that it is very difficult to express in words the horror and pain that occur during times of war and genocide. Sitting next to him and sobbing, his wife added that thirty years after the killings, village burnings, and tortures in Southeast Asia, the world once again faces such atrocities in Sudan.

Although the husband spoke more frequently in class than his wife throughout the semester, she engaged deeply with the course material. In one class session focusing on mixed-race Amerasian children in Vietnam, for example, a Mexicana student asked if the Vietnamese mothers and the American G.I. fathers were typically officially married. In response, after considering various scenarios in which the mother and the father could have encountered each other, the Sudanese female student quietly interjected, "Some of the women might have been raped." When asked if she wanted to say more, she simply repeated her words. Her husband then joined in and repeated the same words once again. Our discussion about stories of war and trauma in Southeast Asia had once again triggered memories of the civil war in Sudan.

Trusting our pedagogies of PTSD in these unscripted situations, we typically follow the moment to enable everyone present (thirty to thirty-five students) to feel the legacies of pain and survival embodied in their classmates' experiences. Rather than retreating from such spontaneous intensity to the distance of assigned readings and projected images, we sit with each other, at times in deep silence, to grieve over deaths and losses while discovering shared meanings of peace, justice, and healing in our education. In sustaining this pedagogical purpose for two decades through the Southeast Asians in the US course, we have necessarily adapted to diverse changing student profiles of our urban public school. This includes a new generation of student veterans from the US wars in Iraq and Afghanistan.

Intersections with New-Generation Asian American Veterans

Extending our pedagogies of PTSD beyond the Southeast Asians in the US course, Tang has designed or adapted several other courses that we describe briefly here because of their effects with student veterans. For Asian American student veterans, in particular, Tang's Asian American Media Literacy course has provided unique opportunities to craft powerful personal narratives in multimedia digital format (Tang, 2010). Originally developed to provide students with intellectual tools to examine critically the political and economic structures of mass media and to confront the impact of dominant representations on individual psyches and group identities, we re-framed students' roles from simply being critical media consumers within their own social locations to becoming purposeful media producers within collaborative spaces of connection and creativity.

The result of each labor-intensive, semester-long process is a collective expression of students' pain and aspiration. At the core of this curricular model is a focus on personal epistemology (Hofer and Pintrich, 2002), informed and infused with pedagogies of PTSD. Students' completed digital stories have focused on family migration, war, health, gentrification, intergenerational communication, body and self-image, homeland ties, and social justice (see, for example, "Wear I Fit" by Pratna Kem, produced in spring 2010; available at: http://www.youtube.com/watch?v=nR1ZW _EAjB4). Students' products—more than 100 of which have been presented to campus and community audiences—are intensely personal, political, positional, and often bilingual.

Several of these recent products represent the work of Asian American student veterans, four of whom served in Iraq:

- A Korean American man documenting the camaraderie invested in his day-to-day training prior to being commissioned as a US Army officer
- A Chinese American woman exploring the intergenerational and cultural conflicts in her working-class immigrant family that led her to leave home and enlist in the Army at age 18
- A Vietnamese American who enlisted in the US Marine Corps, despite the intense disapproval of his father whose own war experience as a soldier in Vietnam had been so painful
- A Khmer American Marine veteran who, after surviving his deployment in Iraq, returns with a deeper understanding of the meaning of "war" for

NEW DIRECTIONS FOR TEACHING AND LEARNING • DOI: 10.1002/tl

his refugee mother who had survived the Killing Fields in Cambodia [available at: http://www.youtube.com/watch?v=CLRWMyyqOU4].

Beyond their documentary contributions in presenting perspectives of contemporary Asian American veterans, these students' digital stories organically reveal multiple, intersecting dimensions of their identities in relation to culture, language, gender, race, immigrant/refugee family backgrounds, citizenship, and religion, together with their critically important status as students and as veterans. Furthermore, their mature willingness to engage fully with our pedagogies of PTSD—whether or not the actual subjects of trauma and healing appear in their own digital stories—supports others to do the same. This is often the case for non-Asian refugees and veterans as well, including in other courses we teach outside of Asian American studies.

Intersections with Other New-Generation Veterans

Tang's general education first-year seminar in American studies, "US Society and Culture Since 1945," for example, consistently attracts veterans and other students from a broad range of backgrounds and political views. Given that issues of war and violence have shaped the personal and family histories and trajectories for many students, this course serves not only to develop students' critical reading, writing, and research skills, but also their capacities for reflection and narrative-sharing through a research project that situates their own three-generation family histories in relation to larger social, political, and cultural events and trends identified in class. Students often know little about their family histories and feel overwhelmed initially by the assignment. After reading examples of family narratives, however, they then relate specific family experiences in the form of spiraling two-minute "interviews" with each other (eight interviews completed in a 75-minute class). The prompts for this activity are

- What are the three most important events in your family history between 1945 and 2010?
- Share one particular story about your family's experience that matters to you or someone in your family.

The interview interactions strengthen students' listening and sharing skills, while also modeling diverse perspectives. In a recent class, for example, a white male student veteran who had served in Iraq during the previous year "interviewed" a classmate about the resettlement experiences of her family which had migrated from Cambodia to the United States in the early 1980s. The structured opportunity to sit face-to-face with each other during this activity enabled them to account for her family's experience of urban racial violence and poverty following refugee resettlement in the

United States and his Irish American family legacy, which includes men of each generation since World War II serving in the US military. In the process, they understood more deeply how changes and continuities in gender roles, social class, migration histories, citizenship status, and political values have defined their personal and family identities, while also enhancing their direct, empathic connections with each other—a key dimension in our pedagogies of PTSD.

Integrative Intersections and Individual Impact

The previous examples represent classroom-specific applications and effects of our pedagogies of PTSD. However, cumulative effects for individual students across courses can be even more powerful. For example, after taking Tang's comparative ethnic studies course, Race, Class and Gender, one particular student, a campus leader majoring in Africana studies, then enrolled in another of Tang's courses, Applied Research in Asian American studies, and became immersed in a semester-long documentary research project focusing on the local Cambodian community in Lynn (Massachusetts), the fifth largest in the United States. The student, who had fled from Somalia with his family a few years earlier, also knew of Lynn, but as one of the sites of recent Somali refugee resettlement. After gaining expertise in documentary research methods, he produced a final project based on bilingual interviews with Somali refugees in Lynn that not only contributed to local multicultural history, but also provided insight about the relationships, interactions, and thematic connections between Cambodian and Somali refugees historically and comparatively.

During the next year while completing his Africana studies major, he took our Cambodian American Culture and Community course to deepen his personal, comparative, and applied understandings of refugee realities. This enabled him to initiate an Asian American studies independent study designed to lay the curricular and conceptual groundwork for what we hope will evolve into the first Somali American studies course at our school, inspired by our shared commitments to pedagogies of PTSD.

In a second example, an Iraqi student decided to complete a six-course concentration in Asian American studies during her final undergraduate semester after having conducted a family history project in Tang's comparative course, American Identities. On her own, she was already actively assisting newly arrived refugee families with obtaining food, clothing, and other daily necessities, as well as providing translation for them to interact with schools, health clinics, and agencies. Through an independent study project guided by Tang, she was able to align her inner purpose more closely with her academic pursuits—writing weekly reflections about her interactions with those families and her own identity as a survivor of the

First Gulf War who fled Iraq as a young adult. She then developed a curriculum about the Iraqi refugee experience, based on the framework of the Southeast Asians in the US course. This process enabled her to link her own identity and experience of war with a longer-term educational vision. A year later as a matriculated graduate student in education and a teaching assistant in Asian American studies, she helped to lead classroom discussions about war and refugee realities. In addition, she worked closely with an undergraduate Chinese American Marine veteran of the Iraq War to co-organize and co-facilitate a story-sharing forum that brought together several student veterans with local Iraqi refugee community members. After this remarkable event, she wrote:

> I already knew that the Iraqi refugees are facing homelessness due to the lack of jobs and the little benefits they receive from the government. But I was surprised at the fact that Iraq War veterans are also facing homelessness, an issue that was raised and discussed by a veteran at the forum. Another struggle the veterans talked about is the instability that they feel as a result of the war. Why are Iraq War refugees and veterans suffering? Why do we deliver people to wars and then act as if they do not suffer? We tend to imagine that they are fine, but the panelists' stories and experiences do not show that they are fine. Their tears do not show that they are fine. In fact, the panelists left the people in the room asking themselves what their role should be to help the affected people, a goal I wanted to achieve (Al-Edanie, 2010, p. 26).

Clearly, this Iraqi student has internalized the pedagogies of PTSD that we practice in Asian American studies, and, like her Somali American peer, she is constructing her own integrative ways to intersect with classrooms, the campus, and communities.

Conclusion

This essay reveals the realities of trauma and post-traumatic stress disorder experienced, in particular, by Southeast Asian American refugee students at one urban public school, and shows how a sustained pedagogical commitment to support teaching and learning with these students in Asian American studies courses has connected meaningfully with newer populations of refugee students from elsewhere around the world and also with a new generation of student veterans who are similarly finding circles of healing for themselves within Asian American studies classrooms and related settings where pedagogies of PTSD are practiced.

Although the literature on refugees' and veterans' mental health typically highlights issues and interventions for these populations within clinical settings (Mollica, 2006), we have found that educational environments can provide alternative, culturally responsive contexts within which some refugee and veteran students are able to reveal the realities of trauma in their lives and make meaningful connections between their past experiences and current or future commitments. Research, documentation, and cultural production with new-generation student veterans—some of whom are themselves children of refugee survivors of the wars in Southeast Asia— are especially important to support and sustain, as are emerging visions for Somali American studies and Iraqi American studies that are being nurtured within our Asian American Studies Program. Such stories and sites of healing have profound meaning and impact, wherever and whenever we are able to share them—including in the content and pedagogy of Asian American studies classrooms.

References

Al-Edanie, W. "Voices Sharing Suffering." *Ripples*, 2010, 2(1), 25–26. Boston: UMass Boston Asian American Studies Program, 2010.
Alleged Gang Fight Results in Death. Boston Globe, Sept. 7, 2003, sec. B2.
Davis, P. *Hearts and Minds*. Film. Los Angeles: BBS Productions. 112 minutes. 1974.
Hofer, B. K., and Pintrich, P. (eds.) *Personal Epistemology: The Psychology of Beliefs About Knowledge and Knowing*. Mahwah, N.J.: Erlbaum, 2002.
Kiang, P. N. "Bicultural Strengths and Struggles of Southeast Asian American Students." In A. Darder (ed.), *Culture and Difference: Critical Perspectives on the Bicultural Experience in the United States*. New York: Bergin & Garvey, 1995.
Kiang, P. N. "Persistence Stories and Survival Strategies of Cambodian Americans in College." *Journal of Narrative and Life History*, 1996, 6(1), 39–64.
Kiang, P. N. "Pedagogies of Life and Death: Transforming Immigrant/Refugee Students and Asian American Studies." *Positions*, 1997, 5(2), 529–555.
Kiang, P. N. "Stories and Structures of Persistence: Ethnographic Learning through Research and Practice in Asian American Studies." In Y. Zou and H. T. Trueba (eds.), *Ethnography and Schools: Qualitative Approaches to the Study of Education*. Lanham, Md.: Rowman & Littlefield, 2002.
Kiang, P. N. "Voicing Names and Naming Voices: Pedagogy and Persistence in an Asian American Studies Classroom." In V. Zamel and R. Speck (eds.), *Crossing the Curriculum: Multilingual Learners in College Classrooms*. Mahwah, N.J.: Erlbaum, 2003a.
Kiang, P. N. "Pedagogies of PTSD: Circles of Healing with Refugees and Veterans in Asian American Studies." In L. Zhan (ed.), *Asian Americans: Vulnerable Populations, Model Interventions, Clarifying Agendas*. Sudbury, Mass.: Jones & Bartlett, 2003b.
Lin, N. J., Suyemoto, K. L., and Kiang, P. N. "Education as Catalyst for Intergenerational Refugee Family Communication about War and Trauma." *Communication Disorders Quarterly*, 2009, *30*, 195–207.
Medaglia, A. "Gun Fires, Dreams Die." *Boston Globe*, Oct. 12, 2003, sec. B1, B4.
Mollica, R. F. *Healing Invisible Wounds: Paths to Hope and Recovery in a Violent World*. New York: Harcourt, 2006.
Tang, S. S. L. "Challenges of Policy and Practice in Under-Resourced Asian American Communities: Analyzing Public Education, Health, Development Issues with Cambodian American Women." *Asian American Law Journal*, 2008a, *15*, 153–175.
Tang, S. S. L. "Community Cultural Development and Education with Cambodian American Youth." In L. Zhan (ed.), *Asian American Voices: Engaging, Empowering, and Enabling*. New York: National League for Nursing, 2008b.

Tang, S. S. L. "Developing Media Literacy for Feminist Advocacy in Asian American Communities." *Campus Women Lead*, 2010, 38(3). Retrieved December 6, 2010, from http://www.aacu.org/ocww/volume38_3/national.cfm

Tang, S. S. L., and Bùi, J. D. "Vietnamese American Community Cultural Development and the Making of History in Boston." In M. Chiu (ed.), *Asian Americans in New England*. Lebanon, N.H.: University Press of New England, 2009.

SHIRLEY SUET-LING TANG *is associate professor of American studies and Asian American studies at the University of Massachusetts Boston.*

PETER NIEN-CHU KIANG *is professor of education and director of the Asian American studies program at the University of Massachusetts Boston.*

NEW DIRECTIONS FOR TEACHING AND LEARNING • DOI: 10.1002/tl

SECTION FOUR

Institutional Change

8

The authors describe a faculty learning community that used intersectional analysis to facilitate critical conversations on the teaching of multicultural content.

From Difficult Dialogues to Critical Conversations: Intersectionality in Our Teaching and Professional Lives

*AnnJanette Alejano-Steele, Maurice Hamington,
Lunden MacDonald, Mark Potter, Shaun Schafer, Arlene Sgoutas,
Tara Tull*

Two decades ago, psychologist Darryl G. Smith (1991) described the enormous challenge and promise of greater diversity in higher education. For Smith, diversity education is a matter of being responsible, as well as responsive to shifting student populations and recognizing the limitation of traditional Western curriculum.

Curricular transformation may be prompted by the diversity of students, but that is not a sufficient motive. The rationale must be that as long as we continue to teach from one tradition only, we perpetuate the notion that, for example, the white middle-class experience in America is *the* important experience and that other experiences provide only interesting anecdotes. The new questions introduced by women's studies in traditional fields—and the revitalization of disciplines that has occurred—are an example of how scholarship and the curriculum can be reevaluated from the perspectives of those at the margin by placing them at the center (Smith, 1991).

The "curricular transformation" that Smith describes goes beyond the integration of new materials that acknowledge the significance of gender, race, class, and sexual orientation. Effective diversity education requires that the instructor be knowledgeable and comfortable with the theories and issues of identity. Given the persistence of curricular ethnocentrism and the highly charged nature of contemporary identity narratives, the preparation of faculty to teach diversity effectively across academic disciplines is no small feat. A robust inclusive curriculum delivered by an instructor who has not come to terms with her or his relationship to identity can be a recipe for disaster. With this challenge in mind, a yearlong faculty learning community (FLC), "Difficult Dialogues" (later changed to "Critical Conversations"), was created in the fall of 2009 at Metropolitan State College of Denver under the auspices of the Center for Faculty Development.

Metropolitan State College of Denver is a large, urban, predominately commuter campus. Throughout its forty-five-year history, its statutory mission has been to provide an affordable baccalaureate education to the residents of the greater Denver metropolitan area. The student demographic of Metro State reflects its urban setting and mission as a college of opportunity. One quarter of its students are ethnic minorities—Hispanics being the largest minority group followed by blacks, Asians/Pacific Islanders, and Native Americans. The typical Metro State student is a first-generation college student who works to support herself, perhaps also a family, while pursuing her studies.

Although Metro State has not pursued an intentional program of multicultural organizational development as defined by Jackson (2005), certain of its initiatives, both past and present, have advanced the cause of a diverse and inclusive campus climate where all individuals "feel fully included and have every opportunity to contribute to the goal of delivering the mission of the . . . campus" (Jackson, 2005, p. 7). The present three-credit hour multicultural requirement, established as a graduation requirement for all students in 1990, is widely perceived among faculty as having improved the campus climate, though both faculty and students increasingly recognize that its focus on ethnic identities rather than intersectional analysis lags behind current theory. The college also has charted an intentional path toward attaining Hispanic Serving Institution (HSI) status. Those efforts embrace strategies for recruitment and retention of students, for creating an inclusive campus climate, for curriculum development, and for faculty and staff development. By working toward these objectives, Metro State is enhancing its infrastructure to the benefit of all learners, adhering to the reminder that "with the growing diversity of our student population, that nice normal curve [that groups most people around a small range of difference] flattens out, so that there are not very many 'average' students anymore—and especially not in open-admission colleges which span the full spectrum of human abilities and human conditions" (Cross, 1999, p. 266). This multitude of difference among both our students and our faculty drove what we thought were going to be "difficult dialogues" in our faculty learning community but instead turned out to be "critical conversations."

Whereas the interest in advancing an inclusive climate at Metro State is widely shared, leadership for this particular FLC, including both co-facilitators, derived from the faculty of Women's Studies. This collaboration between the Center for Faculty Development and Women's Studies is a logical choice because intersectionality is the current state of analysis in feminist theory. Feminist legal scholar Kimberle Crenshaw (1991) and feminist social theorist Patricia Hill Collins (1990) developed this term in the late 1980s and early 1990s to describe the complexities of human identity as not being captured by any single variable—race, class, gender, or sexual orientation. Furthermore, these identities are not simply additive, but interact with one another to create unique experiences. Accordingly, discussions of race as a monolithic experience are limited in value and one cannot, for example, simply add the black experience to women's experience to understand black women's experience.

Intersectional analysis served as the cornerstone for framing the Difficult Dialogues learning community. As the call for participation illustrates (see the Appendix), the co-facilitators sought to balance the personal/experiential dimensions with implications for pedagogy and curriculum. From the outset, this learning community aimed at a holistic approach to diversity education.

Why a Faculty Learning Community About Intersectionality?

Although many people are wary of postmodernism, it helps to explain why a faculty learning community is particularly well-suited to undertake the task of exploring intersectionality in the holistic manner intended for Difficult Dialogues. Postmodernism challenges the notion of categorization and the simple labeling of phenomena. A postmodern analysis is comfortable in the liminal space between categories recognizing their tensions and dynamism (Lyotard, 1984). In other words, postmodernism can often destabilize an idea that was perhaps artificially or superficially thought to be stable in the first place. A learning community destabilizes the classroom in ways that can powerfully engage participants, much in the way that intersectionality destabilizes identity stereotypes. Each allows for a type of postmodern comfort with ambiguity in the service of greater understanding.

Learning communities have come to mean different things to different people and institutions. Truly robust learning communities, however, entail not only a radical departure from traditional forms of education, but also a change in spirit and philosophy. Too often, (student) learning communities are associated with their structure, as in the definition from the Washington Center for Improving the Quality of Undergraduate Education (2010) describing them as "classes that are linked or clustered during an academic term, often around an interdisciplinary theme, and enroll a common cohort of students." Although this description is ostensibly true, it fails to capture the rich implications and potential of learning communities. Traditional education endorses the faculty as the active expert who feeds knowledge into the passive vessel-student. Accordingly, the classroom is the teacher's space, and the course curriculum is under her or his control. Learning communities transform teachers into facilitators and challenge students to take greater responsibility for their own learning as well as the group's learning. For the instructor, giving up control can be disconcerting, particularly given the tradition of well-planned class lectures; however, the potential payoff of student engagement is usually well worth it. Part of the de-centering of the classroom is giving a voice to students and their perspectives. Instead of a focus upon the teacher's voice and experiences, the students' voices and experiences become much more integral to the learning in the classroom through a socialized process of knowledge creation. In turn, the material becomes more personal to the students. Because their voices contribute regularly to discussions, their stories and experiences seep into the class narrative, and they make intellectual connections to their own lives. Accordingly, education theorist Barbara Thayer-Bacon describes this communal approach as both effective and affective in its engagement of more than just cognitive skills. Thayer-Bacon (2000) renames critical thinking in such settings as "constructivist thinking" to account for its participatory approach.

This collaborative form of learning, with a rich history of application to the faculty development setting (Cox and Richlin, 2004), is particularly well-suited for discussing intersectionality because everyone has rich experiences of identity to draw upon. In addition, the sense of attachment found in a learning community creates a safe space where participants can feel comfortable sharing aspects of their personal identity or their confrontations with identity issues. This is particularly important given the socially charged nature of identity concerns that make some people reluctant to discuss them. The Difficult Dialogues FLC had the added benefit of high participant maturity levels and extroversion that comes with the teaching profession.

The co-facilitators issued a college-wide call for participation without any predetermined population in mind. The process of self-selection yielded a gender balance among the ten faculty who signed up but did not result in a racially diverse group (only one member, a co-facilitator, was a person of color). Members included one person each from the departments of Criminal Justice, History, Human Services, Journalism, Spanish, Speech Communications, Theatre, and three from Women's Studies. In addition to gender balance and disciplinary diversity, other dimensions of identity that participants revealed over time included religion, class, sexual identity, and ethnicity. Although participants knew each other's professional status upfront (tenured, tenure-track, and adjunct faculty were represented), expressions of anxiety emanating from the privileges and pressures of their relative status emerged over time.

Difficult Dialogues developed into an idealized learning community. Typically, each two-hour meeting began with an exercise designed to encourage participants to risk a bit of themselves by sharing personal experiences with the group. The co-facilitators assigned short readings that specifically addressed race, class, gender, and sexual orientation; Johnson's *Privilege, Power, and Difference* (2005) served as the starting focus book. It became clear that very little traditional leadership was needed. The co-facilitators planned activities and discussion topics for each meeting, but those discussions typically followed their own organic direction as members eagerly embraced the material. All group members, thus, took ownership of the community in a serious and engaged manner while personalizing their learning processes. The interplay between group and individual dynamics is best exemplified by the change of the learning community's name from "Difficult Dialogues" to "Critical Conversations." During the first meeting of the community, one member suggested the change as a way of acknowledging the need to move from the fear of talking about these issues to the hopeful potential of engaging in meaningful conversations around these topics. The group embraced the change.

FLC Activities and Exercises

A key component of the FLC experience was the array of activities and exercises. These exercises facilitated the creation of a safe space for the participants to reflect upon their personal positions on topics like privilege, racism, sexism, and equality. Many of the exercises were derived and/or adapted from two sources: the National SEED Project on Inclusive Curriculum (Wellesley Centers for Women, n.d.) and *Teaching for Diversity and Social Justice* (Adams, Bell, and Griffin, 2007). For the purpose of the FLC, these activities were adapted to the size of the group and then presented in ways that would be useful in the college classroom. The following is a brief description of the exercises used.

Girl/Boy Essay. Participants read an excerpt from *Girl* by Jamaica Kincaid (1978) and then composed their own "Girl/Boy" essays comprised of gender messages received while growing up. These included both subtle and overt ideas from parents, siblings, friends, families, teachers, and mentors, similar to the messages included in the sample by Kincaid.

Listening Exercise Paired with "Story of Your Name." Participants first reflected upon the origin of their names, its ties to possible family history, nicknames, challenges, etc. The group then shared these reflections in pairs with a restriction of two minutes of speaking time per partner. The exercise is intended to highlight listening fully without interruption, which helps to monitor group dynamics that involve dominant participants.

Paperclip Exercise. Various identity groups (gender, nationality, sexual orientation, race, class, and religion) with a list of privileges and corresponding colored paperclips were posted around the room. As participants read off statements that reflected their experiences, they collected paperclips of different colors with the goal of "quantifying" privileges in a visible manner.

Multicultural Circles Exercise. This exercise included a worksheet with multiple circles with the name of the participant in the center circle. As participants reflected upon their own group membership (for example, mother, Pacific Islander, academic, trapeze artist) they wrote the names of the groups in the surrounding circles. One objective of this activity was to reflect upon in-group and out-group membership, positives and negatives of group membership, and how these groups have shaped the people the participants are today. During paired sharing, partners took turns for each of the following: (1) explaining why their groups were chosen, (2) naming a time one felt proud to be a member of a group, (3) identifying a time one felt uncomfortable/embarrassed being a member of one of these groups, and (4) naming one statement the participant wishes would never be said about one of their groups.

"In the Water" Exercise. Participants provided (positive and negative) "word associations" with race/ethnic-based terms (for example, Asian/Pacific Islander, African American, and so on, but also racially coded terms such as "welfare mother" and "illegal alien"). The purpose was to identify the positive and negative terms associated with each category that are "in the water" to highlight work that continues to be needed around race/ethnic language.

Hip-Hop Beyond Beats and Rhymes. Participants viewed a video clip from the film (Hurt, 2006) to provide visual connection to the assigned reading "Refusing to Be Macho" (Orosco, 2008). The video clip illustrates and defines expectations for masculinity, being "hard," and how rap music enforces gender expectations. Participants learned that sexism and heterosexism are used as weapons by which to put down men who are not "masculine" enough.

"Being an American Means . . ." Exercise. In small groups, participants used markers and crayons to illustrate/list out how they had completed the sentence, with regard, for example, to national affluence, the "American Dream," and the context that surrounds class in our country. Along with this exercise, handouts from the Ruby Payne book *A Framework for Understanding Poverty* (1998) were distributed.

All of the activities helped to build a safe and respectful space for conversations about intersectionality and allowed for individual self-reflection within a larger cultural context. The exercises were necessary to support a community of open sharing. Without understanding commonalities, it would have been difficult to process differences. These exercises contributed to our group cohesiveness that led to respectful discussion and inquiry throughout the year.

The Impact of the Learning Community Experience

At the close of the FLC, all members were invited to share their reflections, both in writing and through facilitated conversation, of their overall experiences. Those reflections inform the findings regarding the impact of the FLC experience.

Personal Impact. As stated above, one of the underpinnings of diversity education is the development of a concept of personal identity. The FLC enhanced this notion of personal identity by incorporating the dimension of awareness of others into the standard definition of self. Affective risk-taking was an essential part of this process, as it led to an increased understanding of a multifaceted personal identity. The readings we prepared and the exercises we performed in the learning community were designed to provide the necessary knowledge for and to construct an environment appropriate to risk-taking. Ironically, as we found when examining our reflections, the shared risk-taking actually created a *safe* environment in which we could develop a heightened awareness of how our individual identities interact with others'. In other words, through risk we discovered safety and intersectionality. The introspective and personal nature of the learning community actually led to improved interpersonal communication. The exercises led us beyond the "touch-feely" and into a shared project of self-evaluation that fostered community for us.

The "risky" activities had an immediate and profound effect on our personal lives. By becoming aware of and then sharing our individual response to the critical conversations that were the crux of our learning community, we were able to involve ourselves in a meaningful way in the emotional, intellectual, and professional lives of our fellow group members. Afterward, one member wrote that, "For me, the most effective part of the FLC experience was the activities and exercises designed by our FLC moderators. Through these exercises, the FLC created a safe space for me to think about my own position on topics like privilege, racism, sexism, equality, etc." This increased self-awareness allowed us to make personal and emotional connections—informed by the intersection of the responses and contributions of our fellow group members—to the sometimes contentious material that we discussed in the learning community.

Professional and/or Teaching Impact. The impact of the learning community on professional or teaching experiences varied. We set out initially to implement and formally assess changes to courses (see Goal 2 in the Appendix: Call for Participants for Difficult Dialogues: Intersectionality in Our Teaching and Professional Lives (Fall 2009 and Spring 2010), but completing that goal did not materialize during the time we spent together. However, changes to our teaching were not insignificant; the learning community gave us a new insight into what it is to be a *part* of the community, not just teach *about* it. One participant wrote that, "In the Faculty Learning Community, we created a microcosm for what we wanted to produce among our students: a truly reflective, honest, safe space for the discussion of ideas that, if repressed for their difficult nature, have more power to harm than to produce social change and justice." In essence, we modeled the transformative activities of both teaching *and* learning that produce a more well-rounded, complete educational experience for both educator and student. Some participants did report an immediate and positive influence on their teaching as a direct result of, for example, preparing a reading for the learning community or participating in an exercise or discussion during a group meeting. As one FLC member explained, "A transformative activity for me was the Boy/Girl exercise. When I openly shared my thoughts and entered into a productive dialog with my FLC peers, I was able to better understand my own values and behaviors, and then I was able to understand how to teach material in the classroom while sharing my own perspective [and] allowing for the perspective of others." This type of "take-away" was for many a crucial aspect of the learning community experience.

Continued Dedication to Life-Long Learning. Regardless of how we varied in being able to identify the direct impact of the learning community on our professional or teaching lives, we all expressed the achievement of a new sense of camaraderie that we believe will be lasting and effective throughout our careers. In our learning community, not only did we learn about each other's field of research or teaching style—we genuinely dug into each other's thoughts and feelings to establish a bond that moves beyond the superficially collegial. As one group member stated, "after participating in the FLC, the sense of community and connection to colleagues and the larger mission that I feel at Metro is invaluable."

It is this invaluable sense of community that leads us to consider future opportunities for critical conversations. When we think about creating those opportunities we recognize that one of the major challenges is bringing a broader diversity of participants to the table. Although our personal experiences convince us of the importance and attractiveness of a "Critical Conversations" FLC, we understand that the sense of safety needed to draw a fully diverse faculty learning community will take time to cultivate.

Our concerns about inclusion do not mitigate the success of this FLC. Perhaps the most profound outcome of the FLC was an enhanced appreciation for perspective and respect as the most foundational tools we can use to enhance the cycle of teaching and learning. One participant captured this well by stating "I believe that holding critical conversations in a variety of settings and with a variety of people is part of the ongoing work to create change and to gain new perspective." We had all started with a common commitment to continue our learning and improve our teaching together. Perhaps surprisingly, however, the cognitive structure of the learning community facilitated an emotional connection, both private and interpersonal, that led to a more profound and lasting impact. We engaged beyond our comfort level, we created a common narrative by contributing our individual perspective, we enhanced our cultural competency and professional satisfaction, and we learned that we could apply the learning community experience to our own lives and professions.

NEW DIRECTIONS FOR TEACHING AND LEARNING • DOI: 10.1002/tl

References

Adams, M., Bell, L. A., and Griffin, P. *Teaching for Diversity and Social Justice: A Sourcebook.* New York: Routledge, 1997.

Collins, P. H. *Black Feminist Thought: Knowledge, Consciousness, and the Politics of Empowerment.* Boston: Unwin Hyman, 1990.

Cox, M., and Richlin, L. Building Faculty Learning Communities: New Directions for Teaching and Learning, No. 97. San Francisco: Jossey-Bass, 2004.

Crenshaw, K. "Mapping the Margins: Intersectionality, Identity Politics, and Violence Against Women of Color." *Stanford Law Review*, 1991, 43(6), 1241–1299.

Cross, K. P. "What Do We Know About Students' Learning, and How Do We Know It?" *Innovative Higher Education*, 1999, 23(4), 255–270.

Hurt, B. *Hip-Hop Beyond Beats and Rhymes.* Boston: Media Education Foundation, 2006.

Jackson, B. W. "The Theory and Practice of Multicultural Organization Development in Education." In M. L. Ouellett (ed.), *Teaching Inclusively: Resources for Course, Department and Institutional Change in Higher Education.* Stillwater, OK: New Forums Press, 2005.

Johnson, A. *Privilege, Power, and Difference,* 2nd Edition. New York: McGraw-Hill, 2005.

Kincaid, J. "Girl." *The New Yorker*, 1978. Retrieved June 15, 2010, from http://bcs.bedfordstmartins.com/virtualit/fiction/Girl/story.asp

Lyotard, J. F. *The Postmodern Condition: A Report on Knowledge.* Minneapolis: University of Minnesota Press, 1984.

Orosco, J. *Cesar Chavez and the Common Sense of Nonviolence.* Albuquerque: University of New Mexico Press, 2008.

Payne, R. K. *A Framework for Understanding Poverty.* (3rd ed.) Highlands, Tex.: aha! Process, Inc., 1998.

Smith, D. G. "The Challenge of Diversity: Alienation in the Academy and Its Implications for Faculty." *Journal on Excellence in College Teaching*, 1991, 2, 129–137.

Thayer-Bacon, B. J. *Transforming Critical Thinking: Constructive Thinking.* New York: Teachers College Press, 2000.

Washington Center for Improving the Quality of Undergraduate Education. "Learning Communities." Retrieved June 15, 2010, from http://www.evergreen.edu/washcenter/lcfaq.htm

Wellesley Centers for Women. "Seeking Educational Equity and Diversity (SEED) Project on Inclusive Curriculum." n.d. Retrieved June 15, 2010, from http://www.wcwonline.org/seed

Appendix

Call for Participants for Difficult Dialogues: Intersectionality in Our Teaching and Professional Lives (Fall 2009 and Spring 2010)

Because issues of identity are infused with personal experiences and beliefs, it is often difficult to talk about them and even more challenging to teach them. Nevertheless, given our cosmopolitan world, the importance of integrating issues of race, class, gender, and sexual orientation into our sphere of understanding and comfort as well as our curriculum is growing. This Faculty Learning Community is an opportunity for faculty to work with one another to better understand the issues and approaches as well as develop concrete teaching methods. As a learning community, the group dynamic and collective interest of participants will dictate the contours of the learning that takes place. The facilitators provide some common material for discussion around power, privilege, difference, and intersectionality, but the participants set the trajectory of the conversation. The lens of contemporary intersectionality theory frames issues of racism, sexism, classism, and homophobia as not isolated forms of oppression, but interrelated and mutually supporting. This is a learning community that is as much about ideas and coming to terms with the language of identity as it is about teaching methodology. The objectives of this FLC are:

1. To develop an understanding of intersectionality and its place in our professional lives.
2. To develop, implement, and assess one distinct change to a class, scheduled to be taught in Spring 2010, that is informed by the themes of the FLC.
3. To cultivate an ability to engage in difficult dialogue with members of the Metro State community.

ANNJANETTE ALEJANO-STEELE *is a professor of women's studies and psychology at the Metropolitan State College of Denver, where she teaches multicultural courses and conducts research on the topic of human trafficking.*

MAURICE HAMINGTON, *associate professor of women's studies and philosophy and director of the Institute for Women's Studies and Services at Metropolitan State College of Denver, is the author or editor of seven books including* Feminist Interpretations of Jane Addams (Pennsylvania State Press, 2010).

LUNDEN MACDONALD *is an assistant professor of Spanish at the Metropolitan State College of Denver, where she teaches language and literature and performs research in the areas of Enlightenment studies, constructivist education, and foreign language teaching methodology.*

MARK POTTER *is the director of the Center for Faculty Development at Metropolitan State College of Denver, where he also teaches courses in European history.*

SHAUN SCHAFER *is an assistant professor of journalism at Metropolitan State College of Denver.*

ARLENE SGOUTAS *is an assistant professor in the Department of Women's Studies at Metropolitan State College of Denver.*

TARA TULL *is an assistant professor and chair of the Department of Human Services at Metropolitan State College of Denver.*

NEW DIRECTIONS FOR TEACHING AND LEARNING • DOI: 10.1002/tl

Focused on comparative ethnic studies and intersectionality, the author commences with a discussion about Barack Obama's historic inauguration and the Asian American literature classroom. Such historical and educational frames foreground a deeper discussion about the possibilities and challenges associated with cross-cultural, cross-racial pedagogies within Asian American studies and ethnic studies.

Re-Seeing Race in a Post-Obama Age: Asian American Studies, Comparative Ethnic Studies, and Intersectional Pedagogies

Cathy J. Schlund-Vials

In 1886, African American educator Anna Julia Cooper told a group of African American ministers: "Only the BLACK WOMAN can say 'when and where I enter . . . then and there the whole *Negro race enters with me.*'" . . . The matter of "when and where," accordingly, is an engendered, enabling moment. The matter of "when and where," in addition, is a generative, transformative moment. The matter of "when and where," finally, is an extravagant, expansive moment. That entry into the American community, however enfeebled by barriers to full membership, parallels the earlier entry into historical consciousness, and the "when and where" of both moments are engendered/enabling, generative/transformative, extravagant/expansive.

—Gary Okihiro, 1994, p. 7

Like ethnic studies initiatives on other university campuses, Asian American studies came to the University of Connecticut flagship campus via racial incident, protest, and subsequent administrative acquiescence. On December 3, 1987, eight Asian American students were verbally and physically harassed while on a bus en route to an off-campus semiformal dance. Despite complaints, state, local, and university authorities failed to address—via punishment and policy—the incident. Consequently, Asian American faculty, students, and community members staged an

NEW DIRECTIONS FOR TEACHING AND LEARNING, no. 125, Spring 2011 © Wiley Periodicals, Inc.
Published online in Wiley Online Library (wileyonlinelibrary.com) • DOI: 10.1002/tl.437

101

eighteen-month protest. In fact, two Asian American professors (Peter Liu and Paul Bok) led a hunger strike demanding redress and the institutionalization of Asian American studies at University of Connecticut (UConn) (Cheng, Chow, and Thomas, 2003). After much back-and-forth, the Asian American Cultural Center and the Asian American Studies Institute were created in 1993 with the express intent of providing on-campus student and academic support. As a joint appointment (in English and Asian American studies) and as the associate director for the Asian American Studies Institute, I am thus the beneficiary and principal administrative advocate for UConn's Asian American Studies Program.

If Asian American studies at UConn was born out of racial strife, it now struggles—with regard to curriculum and programming—to make that history relevant in a post-racial, post-Obama age. Further, the current economic climate makes even more vulnerable units that are ostensibly "not with the times." Nonetheless, this essay argues that courses, programs, and departments focused on ethnicity, race, gender, class, and sexuality remain important precisely because they continue to reflect the asymmetrical distribution of power by way of specific identity politics. Further, Asian American studies—which is critically attuned to "model minorities" and declarations of racelessness—provides a template upon which to deepen discussions of the "color line" and problem of "the colorblind" within the classroom. Lastly, as downsizing hits institutions across the country, the turn toward comparative ethnic studies is a possible solution to the impending crisis of budgetary proportions.

Race and Racelessness in the "Age of Obama" and ENG 3212

Early in the afternoon on Tuesday, January 20, 2009, the nation's soon-to-be forty-fourth president, Barack Hussein Obama, stood on the West Front of the U.S. Capitol with Chief Justice John Roberts. The swearing-in ceremony (the culmination of a two-day-long inauguration spectacle/celebration) set national attendance and global viewing records (Ostrom, 2009). As pundit, politician, blogger, and "person on the street" averred, the election of the nation's first African American president was undeniably historic. Suggestive of heretofore unimagined occurrences and larger-than-life events, Obama's race for the nation's highest office time and again inspired (and often *demanded*) allusions to Martin Luther King, Malcolm X, racial equality, and the Civil Rights Movement. From Hawaii to Illinois, from Kenya to Indonesia, and from a segregationist past to a decidedly more integrationist present, Barack Obama's campaign was at times controversial, incontrovertibly memorable, *and* significantly monumental.

Accordingly, the inauguration's title—"A New Birth of Freedom"—solemnly acknowledged Abraham Lincoln's post-slavery goal of a nation united, establishing from the outset the symbolic stakes for the Obama presidency. At the same time, the notion of "freedom" (and the president-elect's own story of racial uplift and "the audacity of hope") seamlessly intersected with a "content of one's character" sensibility in both Martin Luther King's "I Have a Dream" speech and the president-elect's *The Audacity of Hope: Thoughts on Reclaiming the American Dream* (2006). Correspondingly, Obama's successful bid undergirded allegations of racial progress and signaled the ostensible triumph of multiculturalism, evident in representational equality via the nation's highest office. Indubitably, such multiculturalist discussions were not limited to the U.S. Capitol. Far from Washington, D.C., in the bucolic setting of Storrs, Connecticut, I was about to teach the first class of the spring semester: English 3212, "Asian American Literature." Like so many others, my students and I watched the inauguration, armed with a profound sense of "history witnessing." The frames through which Obama's presidency was principally imagined—redolent of progress, tolerance, and racial unity—and my "inaugural class" experiences structure a tripartite focus on Asian American studies, comparative ethnic studies, and intersectional pedagogies.

An interdisciplinary course, Asian American Literature encompasses more than 150 years of Asian American history, politics, and culture. From the construction of transcontinental railroads to the Vietnam War, from exclusion acts to immigration policy, from "yellow peril" to "model minority," Asian American Literature maps—by means of politics and culture—the shifting terrain of Asian American racial formation. Inclusive of film, photography, and literature, the class centers its interdisciplinary attention on the heterogeneity of Asian America, which includes Chinese, Japanese, South Asian, Southeast Asian, and Filipino writers and cultural producers (Espiritu, 1992). Though the course is open to juniors and seniors, I regularly admit freshmen and sophomores who are interested in taking the course because it fulfills a "diversity" general education requirement. At the beginning of each semester, I have students fill out a short informational survey (which includes name, major, e-mail, and expectations for the course). The course draws students from all disciplines, including engineering, the natural sciences, humanities, social sciences, and education. Despite the course content, most of my students are not Asian American, nor are they English majors. I am the sole instructor for the course.

Returning to the inauguration, my Asian American Literature class was scheduled to begin just as Barack Obama readied himself for the presidential oath. I made the impromptu decision to stray from the typical "first class" lesson plan (e.g., outlining expectations and distributing syllabi). Instead, we spent the first thirty minutes watching the swearing-in ceremony. As the presidential couple descended the platform, I asked students if there was any connection between this presidential "first" and the focus of the course. It was admittedly an unformed question, yet the student response was revealing. In a class of forty-two students, not one student was able to make a connection between Obama's election and Asian American studies.

NEW DIRECTIONS FOR TEACHING AND LEARNING • DOI: 10.1002/tl

Instead, the conversation largely engaged questions of ethno-racial difference. For some, Asian Americans were "model minorities" who had not struggled as much as African Americans. For others, the primary issue concerned "native" and "foreign-born" bodies. Two students brought up the 1992 Los Angeles riots, contending a long-standing conflict between the two groups. This connective absence coexists uneasily with the politics of the 2008 campaign. Though students knew that John McCain was Barack Obama's Republican rival, none could connect the Arizona senator to his infamous anti-Asian campaign slur. In February 2000, the former Vietnam War prisoner of war (then a runner-up to Republican rival George W. Bush) declared to reporters, "I hate gooks. I will hate them as long as I live" (Nevius, Sandalow, and Wildermuth, 2000). This "inaugural student response"—or rather, its lack of connection and connectivity—makes visible the contemporary challenges facing Asian American studies and ethnic studies. Neither field can nostalgically rely on history and memory, nor can Asian American studies and ethnic studies continue to exist in a monolithic racial vacuum.

The Problem of the "Model Minority"

The absence of any identifiable connection by students underscores the problematic imaginary that circumscribes the field of Asian American studies vis-à-vis race and ethnicity. Unquestionably, Asian American studies are uniquely configured around a specific polemic: the "model minority" problem. Since the mid-twentieth century, Asians and Asian Americans have been characterized as an "ideal" minority group. Illustratively, as a Civil Rights–era *U.S. News and World Report* argued, "At a time when Americans are awash with worry over the plight of racial minorities—one such minority, the nation's 300,000 Chinese-Americans, is winning wealth and respect by dint of its own hard work" (Success Story of One Minority Group in the US, 1966). Such "winning" minorities have, within the dominant imagination, achieved socio-economic success via unrelenting labor, perseverance, and—most important—patience.

As the article later elaborates, unlike their "minority counterparts," Asians and Asian Americans have never pushed for political action, are willing to work within the system, and have thus proven themselves "model citizens." Intentionally divisive, the *U.S. News and World Report* article pits Asian Americans against other groups of color, and such model minority frames continue to obfuscate possible connective histories and experiences. All the same, as those in Asian American studies are well aware, the idealized characterization of Asian Americans obscures a very real history of exclusion (anti-Asian immigration acts), discrimination (glass ceilings), incarceration (the internment of Japanese Americans during World War II and the detainment of Arab Americans post-9/11), and war (World War II, the Korean War, the Vietnam War, and the current War on Terror).

New Directions for Teaching and Learning • DOI: 10.1002/tl

In the United States, Barack Obama's election was—as a "matter of race"—mythically cast in model minority frames. Consequently, this native Hawaiian's rise from community activist to president, his patience with racialized attacks (e.g., the Jeremiah Wright "scandal"), and his willingness to work within the political system, echo the tenets of the "model minority myth." Notwithstanding the monumental nature of the 2008 election, one must necessarily recall the precise conditions that *made* (and continue to make) Obama's presidential bid racially "historic." After all, in light of slavery, Jim Crow segregation, African American disenfranchisement, and centuries-long systemic oppression, the election of the first black president was legally, politically, and historically made significant.

Taken together, such model minority frames make Asian American studies particularly relevant with regard to claims of "post-racial America" that accompanied Obama's rise to the nation's highest office. Further, the abovementioned English 3212 class discussion succeeded in addressing what is often seemingly impossible to address: pervasive practices of forgetting and conveniently sutured narratives of closure. With this "recovery" strategy in mind, what ultimately connects Obama's *historic* presidency and Asian American studies is the comparative amnesic segregation of racism to the annals of the "distant past." It is this "past" that my students struggled to comprehend, along with the connective histories between these two groups.

Crossing the "Color Line": Comparative Ethnic Studies

To combat these forgetful frames and disconnected classroom conversations, it is imperative (intellectually, pedagogically, and economically) to seek out *comparative* approaches which bring to light the intersection of race, ethnicity, and nation. Indeed, as Ronald Takaki ([1979] 2005) epitomized, "Like many other scholars, I had parceled out white attitudes toward different groups almost as if there were not important similarities as well as differences in the ways whites imaged and treated them. Yet I knew that the reality of white America's experience was dynamically multiracial. What whites did to one racial group had direct consequences for others. And whites did not artificially view each group in a vacuum; rather, in their minds, they lumped the different groups together or counterpointed them against each other" (p. vi).

If U.S. history, culture, and politics are "dynamically multiracial," they are also comparative, a point made clear in the very characterization of Asian Americans as "model minorities." With this in mind, Takaki's multi-sided and multisited approach provides a new way of "seeing" race and ethnicity by way of "comparative ethnic studies," which unearths similarities, examines differences, and foregrounds connective experiences.

Focused on the historic, relational, and "multiracial," comparative ethnic studies makes legible questions of "why" (e.g., what was gained by discriminatory practice) and "how" (e.g., the ways in which racism was promulgated and perpetuated by means of law, custom, and practice). If Takaki ([1979] 2000) offers scholars and teachers a "why" and "how" analysis, then Gary Okihiro (1994) adds the equally important interrogation of "where and when." To be sure, the question of location ("where") and time ("when") signals a turn toward "engendered/enabling, generative/transformative, extravagant/expansive" teaching strategies. Following suit, these connective strategies challenge students and instructors to go beyond the single-minded purview of race, ethnicity, gender, or sexuality. In the process, Takaki and Okihiro produce a political cartography of ethnic intersections and racial crossroads, which in turn allow for the incorporation of other "why, how, when, and where" moments (e.g., gender, class, and sexuality).

Moreover, Takaki and Okihiro gesture toward an "intersectional pedagogy," reliant on the simultaneous consideration of race, ethnicity, gender, *and* sexuality. Likewise, M. Jacqui Alexander (2005) evocatively pushes intersectionality in stressing that "As we recognize that the nation-state matters more to some than to others, we also need to recognize that the borders of the nation-state cannot be positioned as hermetically sealed or epistemically partial. Our knowledge-making projects must therefore move across state-constructed borders to develop frameworks that are simultaneously intersubjective, comparative, and relational, yet historically specific and grounded" (pp. 253–254).

If, as Alexander maintains, politics are not "hermetically sealed or epistemically partial," the task before "knowledge makers" (and by extension, knowledge producers) is the concurrent movement "across borders" via connective history and comparative subjectivities. The ethnic studies classroom, forged within the fabric of history and politics, necessarily takes on issues of U.S. representation, identity formation, and racialization.

As the field of Asian American studies moves toward comparative frames (e.g., African/Asian American studies, Native/Asian American studies, and Latino/Asian American studies), students (like those in my "inaugural class") by and large are not ready for the conversation. An intersectional approach, which necessarily accounts for connections between power, authority, and identity, destabilizes categories of difference and productively opens up the discussion of systemic racism, sexism, and homophobia. To be sure, this lack of "diversity preparedness" is partially attributable to the historic institutionalization of such programs, which brings to the fore the economic viability of non-comparative schema. Despite the collaborative foundation for ethnic studies, emblematized by the 1967–1968 San Francisco State College strike's Third World Liberation Front (comprised of African American, Latino, and Asian American student activists), departments tend to compartmentalize course offerings in segregated fashion. In this day and age of budget crises, ethnic studies tends to

NEW DIRECTIONS FOR TEACHING AND LEARNING • DOI: 10.1002/tl

fare badly, a point illustrated by a recent *Chronicle of Higher Education* article entitled, "Diversity Takes a Hit During Tough Times" (Gose, 2002). In addition, the direct assault on ethnic studies is multivalent in scope. Legislatively, on May 12, 2010, Arizona governor Jan Brewer signed a bill that prohibited ethnic studies in secondary education curricula. In March 2010, the Texas Board of Education approved the use of a textbook which depicted in conservative and truncated fashion the Civil Rights Movement and downplayed the racial politics of the Japanese American internment.

Hence, notwithstanding Obama's election, administration, and "presidential first," ethnic studies programs and departments around the country are being reconfigured, restructured, combined, and dismantled. Amid recessions, slow economic recovery, and shrinking state budgets, public universities are under attack, a point dramatically evident in mandatory furloughs, faculty/staff layoffs, hiring freezes, and rising tuition costs. As an administrator at a Research I institution, I have witnessed firsthand calls to cut budgets, be mindful of percentages, and be prepared to justify—"by all means necessary"—the program's existence.

Within this dire higher education context, "matters of race" are not financially viable nor fiscally sound in the public university. Over the past year, academic news has been dominated by the impending budget crisis. Indeed, the abovementioned *chronicle of Higher Education* (over academic years 2008–2009 and 2009–2010) has featured several stories focused specifically on the shrinking university. From California to New York, from Arizona to Massachusetts, from research institutions to small liberal arts colleges, ethnic studies is on the chopping block. Ironically, this short sightedness comes when such programs could provide higher education the scholarship and programmatic leadership most required for new models of teaching and learning. What is more, if ethnic studies is represented as economically superfluous, it is concomitantly depoliticized. Such depoliticization uproots the very foundation of ethnic studies and Asian American studies as a significant pedagogical and intellectual site of identity inquiry and critique.

Re-Seeing Race in the Classroom: Comparative Ethnic Studies

An intersectional pedagogy makes possible a "return" to these roots, though it is necessary to commence with vocabulary. Indeed, the legibility of ethnicity and race as complex "keywords" are for the most part eschewed in favor of simplistic tropes of progress (emblematized by Obama's election). The dismissal of "race" and "ethnicity" underscores a widespread, systemic shift in twenty-first century "racial thinking." Correspondingly, if W.E.B. Dubois ([1903] 2005) accurately predicted that "the problem of the twentieth century" would indeed be "the problem of the color-line," then Vijay Prashad (2009) astutely captures the "problem of the twenty-first century": that of the "colorblind."

NEW DIRECTIONS FOR TEACHING AND LEARNING • DOI: 10.1002/tl

To clarify, "colorblindness" is not forged through invisibility or racial "not seeing"; instead, "colorblindness" denies the presence of systemic inequality and privileges "successful" people of color. As Prashad (2002) defines, "This problem is simple: it believes that to redress racism, we need *not* consider race in social practice, notably in the sphere of governmental action. The state, we are told, must be *above* race. It must not actively discriminate against people on the basis of race in its actions. At the dawn of a new millennium, there is widespread satisfaction of the progress on the "race problem" . . . (2002, p. 38).

Within the U.S. classroom, "colorblindness" makes conservative, exceptionalist sense. After all, in a nation founded on "all men are created equal," the dismissal of systemic racism contributes to romantic notions of U.S. nationhood and selfhood. Even so, by recasting the twentieth-century "problem of the color-line" as a twenty-first century "question of the colorblind," Prashad brings to light the central dilemma facing ethnic studies (and even more specifically, Asian American studies) in the celebratory afterglow of Barack Obama's presidential milestone.

To expand, within this "colorblind" milieu, racism and sexism are committed by individuals and not institutions. Following suit, there are racists and sexists but the government, the economic marketplace, and the classroom have been vaccinated (via law and policy) and are now immune to prejudicial power and practice. Accordingly, if colorblind thinking "need *not* consider race in social practice," it still relies on the presence of racial difference as a marker of "progress." Such "progress"—evident in claims of overcoming discrimination and racism—attest to a profound, post–Civil Rights movement shift in the way identity politics have been eschewed in favor of a *flattened* understanding of difference. Put another way, such logic maintains that race is solely a "social construct" that has *eventually* and *inevitably* been dismantled over time.

In turn, this "flattening" underscores the pressing need for different approaches that disrupt conservative multiculturalist readings which obscure and deny systemic inequalities and prejudices. Though Obama's presidency is *historic*, it is by no means the emblem of absolute racial progress. Nor is it the "end" of the Civil Rights line. In light of continuing class disparity, ongoing racial discrimination, legislated homophobia, and still-practiced sexism, Anna Julia Cooper's declaration of "when and where" is *still* relevant. To reconfigure the field through intersectional pedagogy and comparative ethnic studies brings student and instructor back to the politics and progressive histories that make such work pressing and relevant.

References

Alexander, J. *Pedagogies of Crossing: Meditations on Feminism, Sexual Politics, Memory and the Sacred.* Durham, N.C.: Duke University Press, 2005, pp. 253–254.

Cheng, J., Chow, K., and Thomas, P. "Intercollegiate Pedagogy: Possibilities and Limitations of Virtual Asian American Studies," In R. C. Lee and S.-L. C. Wong (eds.), *AsianAmerica.net: Ethnicity, Nationalism, and Cyberspace*. New York: Routledge, 2003.

Dubois, W. E. B. *The Souls of Black Folk*. New York: Simon & Schuster, 2005. (Originally published 1903.).

Espiritu, Y. L. *Asian American Panethnicity: Bridging Institutions and Identities*. Philadelphia: Temple University Press, 1992.

Gose, B. "Diversity Takes a Hit During Tough Times." *Chronicle of Higher Education*, Oct. 11, 2009, Diversity in Academe section. Retrieved May 12, 2010, from http://chronicle.com/article/Diversity-Takes-a-Hit-During/48732/

Nevius, C. W., Sandalow, M., and Wildermuth, J. "McCain Criticized for Slur/He Says He'll Keep Using Term for Ex-Captors in Vietnam," *San Francisco Chronicle*, Feb. 18, 2000, Politics Section. Retrieved May 17, 2010, from http://articles.sfgate.com/2000-02-18/news/17638747_1_mccain-s-words-asian-americans-racial-slur.

Obama, B. *The Audacity of Hope: Thoughts on Reclaiming the American Dream*. New York: Crown Publishers, 2006.

Okihiro, G. *Margins and Mainstreams: Asians in American History and Culture*. Seattle: University of Washington Press, 1994.

Ostrom, M. A. "Obama's Inauguration: Record Crowd Gathers on Mall to Celebrate 'Achievement for the Nation.'" *Mercury News*, Jan. 20, 2009, p. 1.

Prashad, V. *Everybody Was Kung Fu Fighting: Afro-Asian Connections and the Myth of Cultural Purity*. Boston: Beacon Press, 2002.

"Success Story of One Minority Group in the US." *U.S. News and World Report*, December 16, 1966, p. 6.

Takaki, R. *Iron Cages: Race and Culture in 19th-Century America*. London: Oxford University Press, 2000. (Originally published 1979.)

CATHY J. SCHLUND-VIALS is an assistant professor of English and Asian American studies at the University of Connecticut Storrs.

NEW DIRECTIONS FOR TEACHING AND LEARNING • DOI: 10.1002/tl

INDEX